ACHIEVING EXCELLENCE

A Prescription for Health Care Managers

Lawrence C. Bassett
President, Professional Services
Applied Leadership Technologies, Inc.
Bloomfield, New Jersey

Norman Metzger
Vice President for Labor Relations
The Mount Sinai Medical Center
New York, New York

AN ASPEN PUBLICATION®
Aspen Publishers, Inc.

1986

Rockville, Maryland
Royal Tunbridge Wells

Library of Congress Cataloging in Publication Data

Bassett, Lawrence C.
Achieving excellence.

"An Aspen publication."
Includes bibliographies and index.
1. Health services administration. I. Metzger, Norman, 1924-   . II. Title. [DNLM:
1. Achievement. 2. Health Manpower—organization & administration. 3. Personnel
Management. W 88 B319a]
RA393.B34   1986   362.1'068   85-26757
ISBN: 0-87189-277-4

Editorial Services: Ruth Bloom

Library of Congress Catalog Card Number: 85-26757
ISBN: 0-87189-277-4

Printed in the United States of America

To my mother, Genia, who always has managed by common sense, and to my wife, Charlotte, whose common sense always has enabled her to manage.

Lawrence C. Bassett

To my family—ever supportive, ever loving, ever approving.

Norman Metzger

Table of Contents

PRESS ON

NOTHING IN THE WORLD CAN TAKE THE PLACE OF PER-
SISTENCE. TALENT WILL NOT; NOTHING IS MORE COMMON
THAN UNSUCCESSFUL MEN WITH TALENT. GENIUS WILL NOT;
UNREWARDED GENIUS IS ALMOST A PROVERB. EDUCATION
ALONE WILL NOT; THE WORLD IS FULL OF EDUCATED DERE-
LICTS. PERSISTENCE AND DETERMINATION ALONE ARE
OMNIPOTENT.

Calvin Coolidge

A GENERATION OF MANAGERS HAS BEEN TRAINED BY OUR
BUSINESS SCHOOLS TO MAKE MONEY NOT GOODS. GRIPPED
BY A DOGMA CALLED "MANAGEMENT SCIENCE" THE SCHOOLS
HAVE PLAYED AN IMPORTANT INSTITUTIONAL ROLE IN THE
EROSION OF COMPETENCE FOR PRODUCTION.

Seymour Melman

SURVIVAL IN AN ORGANIZATION IS A POLITICAL ACT.

Bacharach and Lawler

Introduction: The Seeds of Success

How does one survive in a paranoid world of health care management? How does a manager or aspiring manager survive in the rapidly changing environment of the American workplace? For decades, books, articles, seminars, speakers, and sages have promulgated concepts and theories, offering management innovations and a plethora of forums, films, and now video cassettes. Somehow, none of these has provided the answer, nor the help that satisfies fully. Textbooks frequently are too long, too sophisticated, or not effectively adaptable to the job. Gimmicky books do not consider the broad range of responsibilities of managers. Surely, something more and different is needed.

This book is the product of nearly 50 years of managing, training, consulting— of doing! It is a management cookbook of recipes that have been tested and retested. It is a survival kit for those who want answers. It is a treasure chest of management gems that work in the health care field; they have worked for us, they have worked for successful managers and leaders, they have worked for politicians and statesmen—and they can work for you.

The book's aim is to demystify management. It shows that management is a logical, common-sense and practical process. It does what textbooks cannot do, in that it puts concept and theory into practical terms. It goes beyond the *One Minute Manager*; it covers what the *One Minute Manager*—and other books like it—leave out. It will enable you to manage yourself, manage your employees, and manage your bosses. Included in this book is a Supervisors' Checklist (Appendix A), a soul-searching exercise directed toward key management personnel in health care facilities. The Motivation Feedback Questionnaire (Appendix B) helps to identify what motivates the employees and the degree of emphasis in order to help the supervisor direct attention to determine organizational and employee needs. Appendix C—Semantic-Differential Test—enables you to look at yourself as your employer sees you.

However, we are realists; we recognize that implementation of our suggestions and recommended approaches may require changes in your normal style and mode of operation. But we have learned that people are not afraid of change. The view that people are afraid of change is a myth, and this book is a shrinker of myths. What people really are afraid of is the impact of change; they are afraid of the feelings of inadequacy, of the ignorance or discomfort, that may come with change. We fear the unknown, the unexpected, the different. We try to avoid the insecurity that may come with change—but we do not fear change itself.

Obviously, there is no point in reading this book unless you do plan some changes, and you are put on notice that you might feel insecure and nervous with a new approach or action. You might be tempted to return to familiar ways, where you are secure and comfortable. Resist! If you see others are made insecure or uncomfortable because you now do things differently, expect it and understand it—but continue. Of course, after you adopt a change, it will not be long before it becomes "normal" and no longer a change.

The health care industry is undergoing incredible and rapid change. It is as exciting as it is bewildering. The manager who is willing and able to change with it will reap an abundance of rewards.

A caveat: things that are simple may not be easy. The game of golf is simple. You need only use a club to hit a small ball into a little hole in the ground; but its very simplicity creates its difficulties. To paraphrase a popular song, we do not promise you a rose garden; we do promise that you can succeed. In our work with thousands of health care managers, we have learned that the only thing that separates the successful from the unsuccessful is sheer stick-to-it-iveness, old-fashioned persistence, and unshakeable determination.

The Peter Principle says (only partially tongue-in-cheek) that people rise to their level of incompetence.[1] We reject it. People rise to fulfill their self-perceptions. Our personal self-fulfilling prophecies determine how far we go and how successful we might be. If we determine something will work, and keep at it and work at it, eventually it will. If we do not believe in eventual success or that we have the necessary abilities, odds are we will fail. Are these the seeds of success? Nearly 50 years of hands-on experience says yes.

Thus, though we do not promise you a rose garden, you can create your own! You can survive while others languish. You do not have to take it anymore!

NOTES

1. Laurence Peter and Raymond Hull, *The Peter Principle* (New York: Bantam Books, 1970), p. 82.

Chapter 1

The Ultimate Carrot: The Art of Applied Motivation

IN HEGEL'S VIEW, WE EXIST ONLY WHEN WE ARE ACKNOWL-
EDGED, AND OUR PRESENT AGE IS CHARACTERIZED BY A
CLAMOR FOR ACKNOWLEDGMENT AS IF NO ONE WAS SURE HE
EXISTED.

Anatole Broyard

1

To many, motivation is like the weather. We talk about it, complain about it, and are frustrated with it. And we may not think there is much we can do about it. Yet we apply motivation and use its principles every day. The problem is our lack of control. Control is a key element; if you gain control, you can use motivation as a tool of power with the employees you manage, with others with whom you must work, and with your bosses upon whom you must depend.

You don't have to be a psychologist or a sophisticated manager to make effective use of motivation. Many managers have not even heard of names like Maslow, Herzberg, Likert, and McGregor. Indeed, when you are under pressure and times are troubled, as they are in today's unpredictable health care universe, there is little opportunity to study theory or concept. What is needed are answers and practical tools that will work for you. (You do not need to know electrical theory when you throw a light switch; all you need to know is whether you can make it work.)

THERE IS NO SUCH THING AS A LAZY PERSON!

People may appear lazy—at times we all do—but appearances mask the dynamics taking place below the surface.

THE PROBLEM: FINDING THE LEVERS OF MOTIVATION

Here is a motivation formula that is as practical as it is real. Understanding and using it will enable you to motivate yourself as well as others. The formula is a triangular path that governs all our behavior:

2

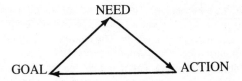

When you have a need (a wish, a desire, a want, a life requirement), it moves you into action.

You stay in action, in one form or another, seeking to reach a goal that will satisfy the need.

Yet action ceases when the need is satisfied, and no action takes place until the need surfaces.

There are no exceptions. Without need, hopes, or wants, we languish, we stop taking action. Without a "need to live," for example, aged citizens confined to lonely nursing homes have been known to cease the action needed to stay alive. Thus, so-called lazy persons, people who appear to lack initiative, are simply persons who, at a particular time, either have no current desires (needs) or do not believe that any action on their part will achieve a desirable goal.

TEST YOURSELF

Imagine your return home at the end of an exhausting day at work. You're sleepy and fatigued; you have to make your own dinner, and you're too tired even to venture out to a restaurant.

1. Would you make an elaborate meal or just something to get by with?
2. Would you bother to do the work you brought home with you if it's not required the next day on the job?
3. How pleasant would your mood be?
4. How eager would you be to do anything that required a lot of physical exertion?

Then the phone rings. It's your boss, telling you that you have an opportunity to work on a special project that could mean a big promotion and a big raise. You're told that you were selected because there is confidence that you are the best person for the assignment.

> (Or, it's a friend. He's just received tickets for an impossi-
> ble-to-get-tickets-for show that you have been eager to see
> but never thought you would. The tickets are for that night.)
> *Ask yourself—"How would I respond?"*
> Probably with enthusiasm and the feeling of exhilaration.
> Your fatigue would disappear and be replaced by an
> eagerness to get into action.
> You tell yourself, "I just got a second wind."

The fact is that the existence of a need or desire determines whether you take action, and what further action you'll take; the strength of the need determines the strength of the action. No matter how fatigued you are, if a need is uncovered that is stronger than your need for rest and sleep, you will go into action to achieve the goal. You return to your fatigued state only after the goal that you seek has been achieved.

> ## COROLLARIES
>
> The strength of the need—the strength of the action. As needs increase or lessen, action increases or lessens.

Examples of the motivation formula at work are in evidence everyday, sometimes quite dramatically. When in desperate situations, people who are eager to stay alive—even rational, educated, highly principled people—often commit acts that might be considered outlandish or even macabre. You may be familiar with the story of the Donner Party. The story was chronicled in San Francisco newspapers and was produced as a television special. A group of American pioneers, during the winter of 1846–47 after spending nearly a year together crossing the continent, were trapped by snow in the Sierra Nevada Mountains. In their attempt to stay alive, they resorted to cannibalism. Their very intense needs produced very intense actions.

Our newspapers and news broadcasts are filled with examples of heroics and seemingly superhuman efforts, such as reports of athletes who surpass themselves under intense competition. Such stories are examples of people who had great needs and took strong action to meet those needs.

The motivation formula explains almost everything we do. The hard-driving employee whose need to succeed drowns out all other interests, the employee who attends night school year after year because of the need to get a college degree, the person who holds two jobs because of a strong need to buy a home—all are commonplace examples.

A study of history is a study of motivation, of the powerful drives that enabled many of the greats to achieve immortality. Julius Caesar's need to become master of the known world drove him relentlessly. DaVinci's drive to learn the secrets of nature and to express his passions in art drove him to many conquests. Columbus's craving to succeed where no other seafarer had before him led him to great journeys. Thomas Edison's insatiable curiosity led him to many discoveries. Henry Ford's competitive drive to sell cars led to the creation of the assembly line. And the masterful effort of NASA to put a man on the moon showed what can happen when a team is motivated to achieve a common goal.

WHAT YOU NEED TO DO

To motivate another, you have to make a deal. You offer to exchange a goal that the person wishes to achieve for an "action" that you desire. If an employee does something well, you make it worth his while. If a person in another department does you a favor, you make it worth her while. It's a barter.

Unfortunately, although the motivation formula is simple, its application is sometimes difficult because we don't know what it is others really want or need. We may *think* we know, but a human being is a very complex organism that hides behind a thick facade, and the facade often prevents others from knowing what it is that makes the person tick. Many of us do not even know our own needs and motivations, and, if we have trouble identifying our own goals, how can we expect to know what it is that others want? How can we find out if they themselves may not be consciously aware of what drives them?

In a health care setting, where there is a wide variety of skills, professions, and disciplines and where there are many men and women working around the clock seven days a week, finding the answers to these questions is critical if we are to motivate our employees or our bosses. If we are to get others to respond to us, we have to uncover the motivators that stimulate action. Motivators come in a variety of forms; become familiar with them:

- *Hidden needs.* At one time or another, we all wish we could do something inappropriate, illegal, or just plain wrong. We have secret thoughts and wishes, and we do not want them known. Yet, some of these needs are very powerful action getters. Many a prominent figure has created a scandal because of a hidden drive, satisfied in a secret life, that suddenly became public.

- *Symbolic needs.* Society has taught us to value status symbols. In *Games People Play,* Eric Bierne describes the game called "Mine is Bigger Than Yours." This is a game that is frequently played in the corporate suite, where the size of an office, the expense of the furnishings, or a title on the door becomes a much sought-after prize. Symbolism is important. In the late 1940s, when television was still in its infancy, many people placed television antennae on their roofs to show their neighbors that they owned a TV, when in fact there was no TV inside the home. In Scandinavia, it is a practice in some businesses to pay higher wages to those whose offices are windowless, since, symbolically, their lifestyles are being diminished. (It has long been believed that money is a principal symbolic need to a worker since the amount of a salary may indicate the worker's status level within the company.)

- *Emotional needs.* Perhaps the most difficult motivations to explain or to deal with are those that are emotional in nature. Sometimes such needs defy rationalization. The desire to get even with a former tyrannical boss has prompted many a worker to tell the boss what an s.o.b. the boss is, even though, for that momentary satisfaction of getting even, the possibility of a decent reference may be destroyed. We do many things, some of them stupid, in which the momentary pleasure we get is outweighed by the repercussions. The strength of the emotional need leads us into an action for which we are later sorry. In the health care setting, the emotional needs of patients are clearly revealed while they are in our care.

- *Changing needs.* Unfortunately, just when we believe we know what it is that makes an employee or ourselves tick, we often learn that it no longer is a strong motivator. Our needs change; they change as they are satisfied, or as something else provides a more powerful incentive. The employee with the reputation for punctuality and high-quality work (to satisfy the need for approval and success on the job) suddenly has a change in value systems after falling in love. The affection of and the need for a mate lead to passions that reduce job performance. Or a highly motivated executive striving to make a sale suddenly loses interest in the sale when faced with a personal crisis.

- *Conflicting needs.* While the strength of a need determines the strength of the action, there are times when more than one need is important. Consider a choice between two jobs, one that offers a good opportunity in a reknowned medical center but requires a move to another part of the country, and another in a local community hospital that is located a few minutes from home but does not offer the same potential as the medical center. Such a choice creates a conflict in needs of many men and women in the job marketplace. Daily, we are confronted with such decisions. We might at times need to decide between two highly desirable alternatives, such as one that means credit for a subordinate and another that might bring some personal glory.

- *Short- and long-term needs.* Managers frequently are asked how they can motivate employees in dead-end jobs. A nursing assistant will never become an RN by merely working hard. And while theorists might offer explanations and conceptual answers, persons who feel trapped do not work up to their full potential. Yet a practical manager can motivate a person who is at a dead-end by providing a continual array of short-term goals, each of which will satisfy some immediate need and propel the person during the day. When you must work on your feet, a pebble in your shoe is a greater motivator than the long-range potential of the job. We are influenced more by the *now* than by the *later*. The proper use of short-term goals or incentives can provide a most effective stimulator of daily increased productivity, cooperation, and initiative.

An understanding of what motivates people is important if you are going to succeed in developing a strong and loyal workforce and maintaining it to assert all of its efforts and imagination to support you. It is also the key element in the decision-making process. If there is any doubt about the importance of understanding and mastering the art of uncovering needs, consider what can happen when those who work for you are unable to attain any need-satisfying goals. Consider the feelings employees have when, no matter how hard they work, no matter how much energy, imagination, and devotion they give to the job, they have no sense of fulfillment, of having achieved the goals they have sought so long.

When an individual is blocked from achieving a goal, the result is called frustration.

The impact of frustration is enormous. One can understand why an organization fails simply by examining the impact of frustration.

TEST YOURSELF

You're waiting for the arrival of a cab to take you to the airport for a flight to an important meeting. The cab is already 30 minutes late. If you miss the plane, you miss the meeting, which can have an impact on your institution's reimbursement. You also might jeopardize a salary increase or a promotion. The time ticks on and still no cab. You are frustrated—blocked from achieving your goal. No matter what action you take—which in this case might include damning the cab driver and pacing and fuming silently—there's still no cab in sight.

How do you feel?

Frustration-anger-hostility-hate. A feeling of giving up, a feeling of just plain helplessness.

The emotions associated with frustration are present in different degrees and intensities, depending upon the strength of the need being denied at a particular time. Every day we are frustrated in some way—an elevator door closes as you are reaching for the button, a traffic light turns red just as you approach the intersection, you learn the person you have called on the phone has just left for a two-week vacation.

On the other hand, managers who are concerned about what motivates others become heros when they provide opportunities for individuals to replace their hostility, hate, anger, and depression with satisfaction and the pleasure that results when goals are achieved.

RETEST YOURSELF

In the midst of your anguish, a friend stops by and offers you a ride to the airport, since he needs to pick up someone.

How do you feel about such a person, someone who relieves your frustration, someone who makes it possible for you to achieve your goal when you had all but given up hope?

The manager who wishes to get the support of others will do so by concentrating on finding out and then delivering on the motivators of employees, peers, and bosses. The degree to which the needs of others are met because of your leadership will determine the degree of effort they will extend to help you succeed. Uncover the motivators in others, and you may have found the principal key to your own personal success.

THE SOLUTION: MOTIVATIONAL FINGERPRINTS

Just like fingerprints, no two personalities are exactly alike. Thus, as you learn to identify the motivational fingerprints (MF) of those whose action you want to influence—subordinates, peers, and bosses—you will gain a level of control and influence that you might never have thought possible. And, as you become a better motivator of others, a more effective reliever of frustrations, your influence and personal success will grow correspondingly. (Incidentally, the use of MF works just as well with family and friends!)

Motivational fingerprints are formed from the compilation of needs, the motivational building blocks upon which a person's behavior is based. You need not be a psychologist to be observant; simply by making a "study" of the individual you want to motivate, the fingerprints will form for you.

Specifically, motivational fingerprints are a compilation of all the information that can be discerned about an individual. When collected, such information reveals the person's pattern of needs and values, which will enable you to understand and identify most of that person's needs, no matter how deeply buried. You then have the basis for designing an action plan to get the person to respond as you wish. Manipulation? Not at all (although you *could* use a promise of needs satisfaction to manipulate). Satisfying someone's needs in return for a desired action is simply a barter system—one in which everyone benefits. A health care manager who is concerned with building a respectful and loyal staff will deliver the promised goals when the requested actions are carried out.

Individual differences between people are more marked than one would expect. Even identical twins, who at first glance appear indistinguishable, begin to reveal differences upon closer study. We are all sensitive to life's clues and cues; we recognize a voice on the phone, we identify someone's handwriting, we detect small changes in attitudes, and we say such things as, "It was unlike him to say that; I wonder what made him change."

In fact, individual differences between organisms are believed by many scientists to explain some of the puzzles of nature. There is evidence that the mother bat returning with food is able to identify her offspring among the hundreds of thousands of other tiny bats by the sound of its cry or individual scent. The Navy finds that, by studying dolphins in underwater research, differences between them can be identified in terms of their preferences. The Navy trainers can then plan rewards based on an individual dolphin's likes and dislikes (a fish, a pat on the head, a tickle on the belly, and so on). Thus, based on their studies, the Navy trainers are able to develop MF for each dolphin. They have discovered that a tailor-made reward system results in better performance.

TRY THIS

1. Give each member of a group (the larger the group, the more dramatic the results) an apple (you can use other fruit as well—an orange or a banana). Ask the group members to study it. Then ask them to note the details and tiny characteristics of "their" individual apples.
2. Have them place all of the fruit in a large basket or box and mix them up.
3. After ten minutes, ask them to see if they can find the particular piece of fruit each of them originally studied.

The results are amusing, but meaningful. Rarely does anyone have any trouble locating the original apple; they spot the individual differences, the design of a blemish, the shape of the stem, the pattern of some markings, and so on.

This exercise works with fruit, but does it work with human beings? How can you determine the MF of your employees?

DO THIS

1. Place on a five-by-eight-inch card the name of each person you want to motivate.
2. List everything you can about the individual:

   - likes and dislikes
   - what brings smiles, what causes frowns
   - what the person likes to talk about; topics that are avoided
   - the type of clothes worn, hairstyle, jewelry preferences
   - the parts of the job done best, and the parts avoided or done poorly
   - whom the person regards as friends, and who are shunned

- all personal details that by themselves may be insignificant but that may become important parts of the final personality mosaic

3. The more information that can be gathered, the better. Therefore, add to your observations as you make them over a period of time.
4. Use information sharing. Frequently it is difficult to observe someone because time, work pressure, or work shifts may keep you apart. In such cases, use an ally who is closer to the object of your study. Get the ally's opinions and views.
5. Analyze the accumulated list for behavior patterns, trends, customs, and habits.
6. Design the motivational fingerprint by listing your conclusions of what the person's needs are, what will bring the best responses, and what seems to get the greatest amount of "action."

If your leadership position brings you into daily contact with employees, you can use an additional tool: the five-minutes-a-day technique. In only five minutes each day with the person, you can uncover motivators and, at the same time, strengthen your relationship, whether it be with an employee, boss, spouse, or child.

HERE'S WHAT TO DO

1. List all those people with whom you have direct contact and whom you want to motivate. Use the list as a checklist.
2. Arrange your schedule so that you can spend five minutes each day with one of those on your list.
3. Arrange to talk with the individual "of the day" for five minutes during work time. (Sitting down and chatting during coffee breaks or lunch does not qualify and is in fact frequently counterproductive, since that's the person's private time.)
4. If it has not previously been your practice to do this, explain to the person what you are doing and why you are doing it. Without such an explanation, the person might wonder "what's happened" and become intimidated.

5. Use the five minutes to get the other person to talk about matters of personal interest. Try to learn about the person's opinions, observations, ideas. Use such questions as:

- What do you think about . . . ?
- How did you like . . . ?
- How do you think we could better . . . ?
- What is your reaction to . . . ?

6. Note your observations on your profile card, and develop the person's motivational fingerprint.

SOME CAVEATS

If it has not been your customary style to spend so much time with the person, the first reactions to obtain an MF will be disappointing. Instead of the person being pleased to talk with you, there may be apprehension and anxiety, even though you have explained what you are doing. The change in the relationship might at first make some persons nervous. They may claim that they "have nothing to talk about" or that there is "nothing on my mind right now." They may even say, "If I had anything, you know I would come to you."

Do not be misled. You may begin to feel that the approach is not workable, and you might be tempted to avoid any further embarrassment by dropping the whole idea. Wait. By the fourth or fifth day, things will begin to happen. The person will begin to open up. Your relationships will improve, and you will learn more about the individual than you ever knew before.

There may be occasions when you have an additional opportunity. This derives from the "tell-a-stranger" paradox, based on the curious fact that

> The less we know someone, the more we talk. The better we know someone the more guarded we are.

For example, if you have a new employee, you have an opportunity to obtain an MF that is optimal as long as you are still "strangers." If you also are new on the job, you have an opportunity that will never be available again.

HERE'S WHAT TO DO

1. As soon after the new employee has been hired, arrange a meeting and conduct a direct interview.
2. Explain that you want to learn about the person's values in order to help ensure maximum job satisfaction for the person.
3. Ask directly what it is that is most important to the person, which kind of work provides the greatest satisfaction, and what rewards the person seeks from the job or career.

In such a situation, the individual may tell you things you will never be told again.

If you are newly appointed or promoted, and *you* are the stranger, proceed as follows:

1. Conduct your own attitude survey. Ask for observations about the job scene or the institution and the kinds of changes or goals each person would like to see.
2. Ask about each person's plans, interests, and values.
3. Ask for suggestions and ideas that would make the department or the institution better.
4. Allow those you talk with to discuss anything of interest to them; they will certainly do so.

The information you gather in this way will not only give you an assessment of the current atmosphere of the workplace, it will also provide you with a good map to follow during your first weeks and months on the job. You will know what employee needs you should strive to address, and your employees will feel you have been responsive to them. Their respect and satisfaction with you as their boss will be translated into better performance on the job—something that will not go unnoticed by your own bosses.

While everybody has a motivational fingerprint, there will be occasions when, in spite of all your efforts, a pattern just does not emerge. In such cases, it may be tempting to give up, but you can't afford to. When all else fails, you can resort to one last technique: the "run-it-up-the-flagpole" approach. While this method should be at the bottom of the motivational toolbox, it might produce results when all else fails. Quite simply, it's a method of experimenting with different incentives until one is found that elicits a response.

HERE'S THE WAY TO GO

1. Make a list of all possible motivations and incentives that you suspect might be applicable.
2. Plan a strategy that allows you to recognize good performance or other positive acts and provide an appropriate motivational response, for example, verbal recognition, a word or letter of commendation, a desirable assignment, some extra time off, and so on.
3. Note the reaction and response. Evaluate whether the reaction was enthusiastic or "bored."
4. If a particular motivation appears to work, test it by finding opportunities to repeat it.
5. Build on what you know until you finally understand what it is that will bring the desired response.

If this approach doesn't work, you may conclude that the person's needs cannot be satisfied in the workplace. This is not a defeat or a recognition of inability to motivate. It is merely an explanation of why the performance or attitude is less than the person is capable of. In such cases, the next best course would be to coach and counsel. In a discussion, bring to the surface the fact that you are willing to help the person find job satisfaction, but that the person's cooperation and understanding will be necessary. In many cases, an employee will feel relieved when a well-intentioned supervisor points out the limitations of a job that prevents the employee from achieving personal goals. Be cautious, though. When handled abruptly or roughly, an employee may believe you just want to find a replacement, not work with the employee to increase motivation.

Keep in mind that a plan of action can be designed for those to whom you report as well as for those who are on your own level. Providing a "reward" to a fellow supervisor when you get cooperation and reinforcing the behavior of a boss by conveying a compliment for something that is handled well are excellent ways of improving the odds that the desirable behavior will be repeated and that you are perceived in a positive and constructive light.

You can also find your own motivational fingerprints. Many of us are not certain what we want from our jobs or lives. We are caught in a rut and find little satisfaction in what we do. In such situations, we can uncover our own motivational fingerprints by following the same procedures we apply to others. Describe and listen to your own likes and dislikes. Identify those things that turn you on or turn you off. In this way, you can reveal patterns that you will recognize as self-motivators.

If you find yourself in a situation where your boss is not inspired to motivate you, where there is little incentive for you to improve your performance, and hence you are in danger of falling into mediocrity, use self-motivation to stimulate yourself.

FOR SELF-MOTIVATION, TRY THIS

1. Make a list of rewards, tangible and intangible, that you would enjoy receiving (a piece of jewelry, an electronic gadget, a dinner in a restaurant, tickets to a show or baseball game).
2. List the rewards in order of value and importance.
3. Let someone close to you know your plan of action. If possible, buy the item but give it to the other person to hold. Letting someone else know your plan and keep the reward from you will help prevent you from going back to old habits, since you are now challenged by having someone else watching you.
4. As you achieve the objectives or accomplish the tasks that required the extra effort, reward yourself according to the value of your accomplishment. Now you can enjoy the reward because you've earned it.
5. If possible, get a group of people involved. In this way, a productively competitive atmosphere is created and enhanced.

Caution: Even dolphins don't get rewarded every time.

In fact, too many rewards make the achievement of a goal less satisfying. Just be sure that you are able to taste the fruits of success frequently enough to feel continually the warm glow of accomplishment.

So it is with others. When subordinates, bosses, peers, and friends know that the chances of getting a reward from you are good, that will be sufficient to keep their level of satisfaction—and respect for you—high. The carrot is a powerful tool!

Chapter 2

The Emperor's New Clothes: Tell Them What They Want To Hear

COMPETITION FOR THE GOODWILL OF THE LEADER OR PRI-
MAL FATHER FOLLOWS THE PATTERNS DESCRIBED BY FREUD,
EXCEPT THAT ENVY GENERATES ESPRIT DE CORPS WHICH, IN
TURN, GENERATES GREATER ENVY. THE HORDE BECOMES A
MASS, MEN NOT ONLY PERMIT THEMSELVES TO BECOME A
MEANS, THEY SEEK THEIR OWN DEBASEMENT IN THE HOPE OF
WINNING SECRET FAVORS.

Earl Shorris

2

When was the last time you told your boss what you really think of him? When was the last time you told your boss about major problems in the organization, without coloring the report? Someone once quoted the following pronouncement from a newly replaced hospital director to his replacement: "Yesterday was the last day you heard the truth from your subordinates."

FIVE REALITY QUESTIONS

1. To what extent do you make decisions based upon how happy it will make others?
2. To what extent do you avoid making decisions because you are afraid it might upset others?
3. To what extent do you play "pass the buck" rather than take responsibility for things if you are afraid people will become upset?
4. To what extent do you avoid telling others things that would be of help and value to them but you are afraid they may become angry or upset at your frankness?
5. To what extent do you have an obsessive worry about how much others love you?

The desire for approval of one's superiors and subordinates is pervasive in the American work arena. We want to be acknowledged. We want to be loved. We want to be appreciated. And, in order to be these things, we often have to curry favor and, most of all, not rock the boat. Too often, supervisors screen out communications to their superiors that in any way might redound to their discredit. In fact, as noted above, the truth is often carefully colored by one's subordinates. They learn how to play the game, to tell their superiors what they think their superiors want to hear. This phenomenon—"the emperor's new clothes" s. 1-drome—is also nurtured by superiors who wish to clone the organization with their own "boys and girls."

Several philosophers have pointed to the enormous pressures in our society to win the approval of others. It has been said that our present age is characterized by a clamor for acknowledgment, as if people weren't sure they existed. In order to be loved, we often do things that we know are wrong. In order to be accepted, we adopt styles that are alien to our better instincts.

Many organizations encourage this selling of the self. The boss establishes an acceptable style, which then becomes the pervasive one throughout the organization. Sadly, many health care managers also adapt or sell out. Too often, instead of creative management we have a bland form of management whose hallmark is sameness. The boss often establishes the style of the day. If the boss smiles, everyone smiles; if the boss frowns, everyone frowns; if the boss acts irrationally, the irrational behavior is often passed down the line in a scapegoating chain. We try to agree with our bosses and attempt to make their prophecies work, even if they are false and counterproductive. There the boss stands with no clothes on, and we'll tell him that his new tailor has produced the most stylish adornment. *The emperor's new clothes tailored anew in American management.* We tell our bosses what they want to hear; we make ourselves look good in their eyes, even if it means sacrificing the interests of the people with whom we work or the people who work for us.

> Organizations are peopled at times with leaders whose sole purpose is to enhance their positions and careers no matter who is negatively affected.

It is up to you to keep your head attached to your heart. Most health care organizations tend to hire managers by a system called "cloning." They want employees on the management team to "fit" into the organizational pattern. All the more the pity, since those who are "different," those who are "boat rockers," may be far better for the organization than those who filter information and tell their bosses only what they want to hear. Are you a communication filter? A communication barrer? A rubber stamp? If you wish to succeed in the highly politicized work arena in our country, you must first establish a bifocal view of success: To succeed, you must meet the goals of the organization, and you must also meet your own goals. If you sacrifice the latter for the former, the price will become obvious as time passes—you will learn to hate the organization; you will learn to hate your boss; and you will learn to hate yourself. Consider the following sad commentary on the ease of "learning to hate" in our work lives:

> We can establish our basic organismic footing with hate as well as submission. In fact, hate enlivens us more, which is why we see more intense hate in weaker ego states. The only thing is that hate, too, blows the other person up larger than he deserves.
>
> *Ernest Becker*

There is no payoff in hating the boss; there is less payoff in hating yourself. You must gain, not erode, your self-respect. To do this, you must be—to use a trite expression—true to yourself. There is in our society a growing employee dissatisfaction, which must be, in part at least, a result of the lack of self-respect and of the concomitant lack of appreciation for one's contribution at work.

More and more, reports indicate that employees' faith in the ability of top management continues to plummet. These same reports indicate that top management is becoming more and more isolated from the workforce. How can you become less isolated from the people who work for you and feel better about yourself in your relationship with your boss?

> It's time to tell the boss that he has no clothes on.

> Let's stop at this point and take a short test. Check either "usually," "sometimes," or "never."
>
> 1. I've gone home after work and muttered to myself, "I should have told him this or that."
>   Usually ___ Sometimes ___ Never ___
> 2. I sit in my office after a meeting and think, "If I only had . . ."
>   Usually ___ Sometimes ___ Never ___

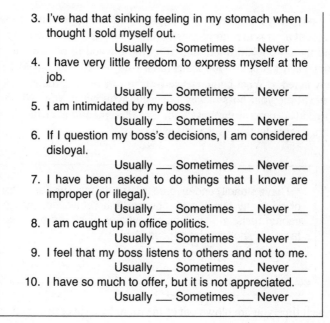

3. I've had that sinking feeling in my stomach when I thought I sold myself out.
   Usually ___ Sometimes ___ Never ___
4. I have very little freedom to express myself at the job.
   Usually ___ Sometimes ___ Never ___
5. I am intimidated by my boss.
   Usually ___ Sometimes ___ Never ___
6. If I question my boss's decisions, I am considered disloyal.
   Usually ___ Sometimes ___ Never ___
7. I have been asked to do things that I know are improper (or illegal).
   Usually ___ Sometimes ___ Never ___
8. I am caught up in office politics.
   Usually ___ Sometimes ___ Never ___
9. I feel that my boss listens to others and not to me.
   Usually ___ Sometimes ___ Never ___
10. I have so much to offer, but it is not appreciated.
    Usually ___ Sometimes ___ Never ___

If your answers to these questions were all "never" you can move on to the next chapter; you are, indeed, a very unusual manager, working in a very unusual environment. Move on to the next chapter with a smile. If, on the other hand, you have several "sometimes" and several "usuallys" (or, God forbid, many "usuallys"), then it is best that you continue to read this chapter.

It is interesting to note that Daniel Yankelovich, a social scientist who has conducted many important surveys, found that an overwhelming 84 percent of all Americans "feel a certain resentment: a belief that those who work hard and live by the rules end up on the short end of the stick."[1] In a recent speech, he quoted a University of Michigan study that, over a 20-year span, found a doubling of the number of people who consider their jobs to be a source of unhappiness. He added that "only 13 percent of all working Americans find their work truly meaningful and more important than their leisure time pursuits."[2] Too often, we spend our working days in competition for the goodwill of the leader. In attempting to win the favor of the leader, we indulge in self-debasement. If we remain silent, do not offer criticisms, or refute obvious factual errors and instead just obey, we have no identity. We normally do not act that way at home. In many instances, we manage our family lives better than we do our work lives. We argue with our mates and point out the foolishness of our neighbors. We advise and we decide; we are adults. Why then must we act as children in the workplace? Why must we agree with the person who says that the blue item is green?

One study of the problem of workplace discontent concluded that what the workers want most is to become masters of their environments and to feel that both they and their work are important. It's time for you to become master of your environment. It's time for you to heighten your self-respect. As M.P. Follett has so wisely noted, "What heightens self-respect increases efficiency."[3]

The next time your boss makes a decision with which you disagree, gently—ever so gently—present the boss with facts designed to alter the decision. Give your boss a reproduction of the following:

> I have steadily endeavored to keep my mind free so as to give up any hypothesis, however much beloved, (and I cannot resist forming one on every subject), as soon as facts are shown to be opposed to it.
>
> *Charles Darwin*

The next time you are blown out of the room by a superior's irrational position or unwillingness to face up to the truth, read the following quietly to yourself and put the whole thing in proper perspective:

> It does not worry him that his "ideas" are not true, he uses them as trenches for the defense of his existence, as scarecrows to frighten away reality.
>
> *José Ortega y Gasset*

If in the face of irrational behavior, you have tried, you have called a spade a spade, you have come to recognize what is real and what is sham, your integrity will not be submerged. If, on the other hand, you continue to bury your creativity by submitting, you will wither away, both as a leader and as a human being. Michael Maccoby describes the dilemma in the following words:

> He needs to be liked and accepted by strangers in order to gain a livelihood. The danger for him is not so much that he will harden his heart, but that he will lose his integrity, sense of self-esteem, and value in an attempt to adapt and ingratiate, to be what others want, to become more marketable.[4]

You can contribute more. As Willy Loman's wife said in *The Death of a Salesman,* "Attention must be paid." It is essential that you assert yourself—not in an obnoxious, oppressive manner, but rather in a quiet but forceful presentation.

> I am an important member of the team. I have much to contribute. I should be heard. I will cooperate, but I will not sacrifice my integrity nor my being.

It is time to gently rock the boat. It was a little child who told the emperor, "You are standing naked." The emperor was relieved and pleased to hear the truth!

To build up an environment of trust,[5] one has to define one's own values within the context of the work arena. In a survey conducted by the American Management Associations, the personal qualities managers admire most in themselves and in others were shown to be responsibility and honesty.[6] There is a payoff to those who cherish responsibility and honesty and, of course, integrity. Early on in our careers, we make a choice as to whether or not we will submerge our own values, if they differ from the organization's, into the organizational matrix. Survival is the rationalization for such submersion. If, as Freud has told us, man's touch with reality is in his work, then we must find *meaning* in our work. All is lost if there is no meaning.

> If we hope to live not just from moment to moment . . . then our greatest need and most difficult achievement is to find meaning in our lives.
>
> *Bruno Bettelheim*

The supervisor's survival kit is more than a kit for surviving in the workplace; it is a kit for surviving *in life*. Increasingly, studies are pointing out that managers' job satisfaction is declining. It is not only managers' satisfaction with pay that is declining. More importantly, the dissatisfaction reflects a concern with managers' inability to make meaningful contributions, to be acknowledged and to be heard. *Surviving is not enough.* Managers have a need to be productive, to take pride in their work, not to be demeaned or overlooked.

Many years ago, a young man entered an office in which one of the authors was working. The man had a package to deliver. It was a busy office. The man attempted to get the attention of one of the people at a desk near the entrance, but the person paid little attention to him, saying, "You'll have to wait, I'm much too busy at this time." The man was persistent, but was rebuffed again by the person at the desk, who said, "I can't take the time. You'll have to wait." Puffing himself up, the young man shouted out, "My job is important! Please pay attention!"

Not everybody can walk around with a stethoscope around the neck, or with an ID badge with vice president printed on it. Few can wear the crown of an emperor, yet *attention must be paid*!

At times you may feel that you are nothing in the organization. This is not true! One can look at one's life either as a half full glass or as a half empty glass. *Possibility* is the watchword; you must grasp the possibilities! The problems of the organization will not fade away when you reassert your feeling of the possible; they will still be there. But you will now feel better about yourself. Occasionally, rocking the boat is good for the soul. Occasionally, saying, "I prefer not to," leads to a whistling on the way home.

The desire for constant approval from one's superiors and subordinates, the need not to rock the boat, the filtering of information that may disturb one's superiors, the submersion of one's needs by "playing the game "—all of these lead to weak supervision. And there is no question that weak supervision is one of the primary causes of poor employee morale.

Very often, weak supervisors are not supportive of subordinates. They may be politically sophisticated; in fact, it has been demonstrated that many weak supervisors are consummate company politicians. Yet all too often such behavior results in a debilitating work and life style. Passive and submissive supervisors produce poor subordinates. On the other hand, a positive chain reaction can flow from strength and individual identity.

> Self-reliant, trusting and decisive supervisors produce efficient subordinates. In the daily competition for employees' allegiance and loyalty the strongest and most aggressive and decisive representative will nearly always win out.
>
> *Robert N. McMurry*

What is needed now on the American work scene is not a yearning for the Japanese model but competent management leadership—leadership that employees will recognize as caring about both the economic well-being of the company and the needs of employees. From this will spring trust.

The great management minds keep telling us that we must build from the top down. This is not always true! For those of you who have fought the good battle and still can't seem to get an answer, the best way to become involved in top management decision making is to involve your subordinates. You must provide opportunities for your subordinates to make decisions. You must build up confidence by displaying your integrity and concern. When, in this way, you build up an efficient departmental operation, the boss is going to stand up and take notice.

There is in fact such a thing as bottom-up pressure for management change. If you are a nonthreatening and supportive leader, you will create an attractive work environment and develop a sense of commitment in your subordinates that will "gently rock the boat"—and bring meaning into your worklife. It is not enough to tell the emperor that he is naked, or to occasionally say, "I prefer not to." *It is time to reassess your values.*

WHAT I BELIEVE

- I shall treat my subordinates as adults. I shall give my subordinates "elbow room." I shall appropriately acknowledge the good works of my subordinates. I shall encourage excellence.
- I shall share to the fullest extent decision making with my subordinates.
- I shall encourage diversity.
- I shall not pass the buck. I shall make my subordinates feel good about themselves.
- I shall reach out every day in every way to touch my employees, to make them understand that I care.
- I shall not scapegoat.
- I shall not corner the market on credit—I shall share it.
- I shall work toward the erosion of the rigidity and authoritarianism in my organization; I shall gently but persistently rock the boat.

When people think of someone as Machiavellian, they refer to the type of wily leader described by Niccolo Machiavelli. There continue to be negative interpretations attached to such leadership behavior. On the other hand, Machiavelli warned the Prince to beware of flatterers: "There is no other way of guarding one's self against flattery than by letting men understand that they will not offend you by speaking the truth."[7]

The search for honest and unfiltered advice from your subordinates is complicated if you are a "secret" person. Again, to quote Machiavelli,

As the Emperor is a secret man he does not communicate his desires to anyone or take any advice, but as on putting them into effect they begin to be known and discovered, they begin to be opposed by those he has about him, and he is easily diverted from his purpose. Hence it comes to pass that what he does one day he undoes the next, no one ever understands what he wishes or intends to do, and no reliance is to be placed on his deliberations.[8]

This was not mischievous advice; you must build up a relationship with your subordinates that compels them to be honest with you.

Let us conclude with some final words from Machiavelli: "And it cannot be otherwise, for men will always be false to you unless they are compelled by necessity to be true."[9]

NOTES

1. Daniel Yankelovich, Address to the National Conference on Human Resources, Dallas, Texas, October 25, 1978.

2. Ibid.

3. M.P. Follett in a paper presented in 1925.

4. Michael Maccoby, *The Leader, A New Face for American Management* (New York: Ballantine Books, Random House 1981).

5. William Ouchi defines trust as consisting "of the understanding that you and I share fundamentally compatible goals in the long run, that you and I desire a more effective working relationship together, and that neither desires to harm the other" (William Ouchi, "Going from A to Z: Thirteen Steps to a Theory Z Organization," *Management Review*, May 1981: 9).

6. Warren H. Schmidt and Barry Z. Posner, *Managerial Values and Expectations* (New York: AMA Membership Publications Division, American Management Associations), 34.

7. Niccolo Machiavelli, *The Prince* (1513; New York: Bantam Books, 1981), Chapter 23, 81–82.

8. Ibid.

9. Ibid.

Chapter 3

People Need To Know You Care: The Cornucopia of Fruit

OUR GENERAL OBSERVATION IS THAT MOST MANAGERS KNOW VERY LITTLE ABOUT THE VALUE OF POSITIVE REINFORCEMENT. MANY EITHER APPEAR NOT TO VALUE IT AT ALL, OR CONSIDER IT BENEATH THEM, UNDIGNIFIED, OR NOT VERY MACHO.

Thomas J. Peters and Robert H. Waterman, Jr.

3

Late one evening, a scientist rushed into the president's office with a working prototype. Dumbfounded at the elegance of the solution, and bemused about how to reward it, the president bent forward in his chair, rummaged through most of the drawers in his desk, found something, leaned over the desk to the scientist, and said, ''Here!'' In his hand was a banana, the only reward he could immediately put his hands on.

Thomas J. Peters and Robert H. Waterman, Jr.

POSITIVE REINFORCEMENT THAT MOVES PEOPLE

Not everybody will appreciate a banana, but everyone will appreciate the symbol of immediate and positive recognition of a job well done. Over the decades, researchers have looked for the answer to the puzzling question of what employees need most? Surprisingly, the answer does not vary from year to year— It is consistently ''full appreciation for work done.'' On the negative side of the question, ''What is the greatest fear,'' all of us continue to be surprised by the enormous reaction to criticism, which turns out to be one of the greatest fears of human beings. Like you, the people who work for you want to know where they stand. The once-a-year performance evaluation program that your institution may have is a far cry from the recognition we're talking about here.

Immediate positive recognition is a necessary stimulus for continued efficiency.

Let's say one of your employees makes a contribution, does something right, and you have seen and recognize the accomplishment. If, following the advice of the behavioral scientist B.F. Skinner, we reward such an employee, it is likely that such behavior will be repeated. Indeed, the higher the value of the reward, the more likely the behavior will be repeated.

When was the last time your boss told you that you were doing a good job? When was the last time you did something well and it was immediately recognized? That feeling of elation—which is not uncommon in such instances—is what positive reinforcement is all about. It is not the once-a-year increase in our salaries. It is not the once-a-year conversation that goes on at performance review time.

> Find out the "fruit of choice" and hand it out to those who excel. One person's banana is another person's tangerine.

In order to identify the relevant "fruit of choice," you must know your employees. You must know as much as possible about their personalities, their needs, their fears, and their expectations. These are not the same for all employees working for you. Thus, you must get to know your employees as individuals. This takes time. The process should be neither hastened nor feared. The people who work for you bring to health care a myriad of traits, characteristics, and emotions. Each individual differs from the next one. You must identify the individual personalities and recognize that, notwithstanding the differences, most people want to feel important; they have a burning desire for the approval of others, and a deep resentment of criticism.

> The lesson to be learned from the behavioral scientists and from your own experiences is that, to succeed as a supervisor, you must treat the individual *as an individual.*

EMPLOYEES' NEEDS

Among the many surveys of employees' needs, the earliest was conducted in 1946. Here are the results:[1]

WHAT PEOPLE WANT FROM THEIR WORK
(1946)

Employee Ranking		Supervisor Ranking
1	Full appreciation of work done	8
2	Feeling of being in on things	9
3	Sympathetic help with personal problems	10
4	Job security	2
5	Good wages	1
6	Interesting work	5
7	Promotion and growth in the organization	3
8	Personal loyalty to employees	6
9	Good working conditions	4
10	Tactful discipline	7

Recently, Kovach used the same 1946 questionnaire with a group of over 200 employees and their immediate supervisors to see whether needs had changed dramatically in the intervening years. He found these results:[2]

WHAT PEOPLE WANT FROM THEIR WORK
(Present)

Employee Ranking		Supervisor Ranking
1	Interesting work	5
2	Full appreciation of work done	8
3	Feeling of being in on things	10
4	Job security	2
5	Good wages	1
6	Promotion and growth in the organization	3
7	Good working conditions	4
8	Personal loyalty to employees	7
9	Sympathetic help with personal problems	9
10	Tactful discipline	6

Source: Reprinted by permission from *SAM Advanced Management Journal*, Spring 1980, "Why Motivational Theories Don't Work," by Kenneth A. Kovach.

Clearly, full appreciation of work done is still one of the most important needs expressed by workers.

> If you wish your merit to be known, acknowledge that of other people.
>
> *Old oriental adage*

In the early survey, as in the recent one, supervisors view good wages and job security as critical needs of their subordinates; and they underestimate the importance of full appreciation, interesting work, and a feeling of being in on things. It is of course essential that you recognize that your subordinates are individuals, that you get to know them as human beings as well as workers. It is, however, equally important to understand the enormous significance of recognition. Whether with a banana or a tangerine, with a pat on the back or a smile, it is essential that you acknowledge, both to them and in public, their accomplishments. This satisfies the key need for recognition and for feeling important. It helps employees believe that they are accepted and approved by the institution and by their supervisors. It shows them how and why they are doing useful work. And it tells them that you know of their contribution.

EVALUATING PERFORMANCE

Increasingly, research is indicating that work performance improves appreciably when employees know what results are expected and when they are doing well. Your subordinates must know what is expected of them on the job day to day, and they must know when they are meeting your expectations. Kessler has listed some of the more important points in the critical management process of performance evaluation:

1. Work performance is improved appreciably when the employee knows what results are expected. Work planning and review sessions provide the individual with information as to the results expected, the methods by which they will be measured, the priorities, and the resources available.
2. Work performance is improved appreciably when the employee knows that it is possible to influence the expected results. The process is sufficiently flexible to permit the individual to have some say about the results expected, the methods by which they will be

measured, and the priorities. The degree of influence the employee exercises will vary according to the situation.

3. Knowledge of results may be as precise and specific as possible. Work review allows the subordinate and the manager to review the results against the goals.
4. Knowledge of results must be as immediate and relevant as possible.
5. Knowledge of results that comes from the individual's own observations is more effective than that obtained from someone else's.[3]

> The successful supervisor is able to communicate to employees who have performed below standard and is interested enough to commend those who have obtained above standard performance.

Your employees want to know what you and the institution expect of them. Certainly our doctors know what is expected of them. Other employees also want to know when they are doing well and when they are not measuring up to expectations.

Unfortunately, the need to know which areas require improvement is often suppressed by employees because of *the way* such information is communicated to them. If such information is presented properly—with a view toward improving rather than punishing—it will be far more effective than the often punitive presentation of negative performance. Most supervisors and managers dislike and question the necessity to criticize subordinates' work. Many of them think it is easier to say nothing. Yet *supervision* must mean just that: the manager is responsible for the performance of others, and therefore must periodically communicate the results of such performance.

Merrihue has observed that the supervisor who obtains the best from employees is the one who creates the best atmosphere or climate of approval within which the work group operates. The supervisor accomplishes this by:

- developing performance standards for the employees, and setting them high to stretch the employees
- measuring performance against those standards
- consistently commending above-par performance
- letting employees know when they have performed below par[4]

You should look at any formal performance evaluation program as part of a plan to enable your subordinates to progress, not as a means to impose conformity or to convey criticism.

> Supervisors should inspire improvement and develop a plan to help individual workers become more efficient.

It matters not at which level one is performing in the health care organization; at all levels, *people want to know where they have been, where they are now, and where they are going.* All members of the organization want to know exactly what the organization, and specifically their bosses, expect them to do; many want to learn what is expected of them in order to move up in the organization. Positive reinforcement—immediate recognition—signals to subordinates that they are on the right track.

A PLAN FOR EXCELLENCE

It is essential to understand that you have available to you as management tools both positive and negative reinforcement. A substantial body of evidence has directed our attention to the use of positive reinforcers, which are deemed to be more consequential in producing appropriate behavior in the workplace. But, in attempting to select the appropriate reinforcement, remember that individuals differ in as many ways as they resemble each other.

> What one person regards as a rewarding experience may be regarded by another as neutral or nonrewarding or even punishing.
>
> *N. McGeehee and P.W. Thayer*

Reinforcement (rewards or recognition) is most effective when it is immediate. The banana mentioned in the opening anecdote may have been more effective than one might imagine: It was a sign of recognition, the best that the president could give the employee at the time; and it was recognized as such. Timing is essential when you are providing recognition. The reason that once-a-year increases fail as long-term motivators is that they are far removed from the highlights of the individual's performance during the year.

An interesting example of reinforcement has been reported by Hildum and Brown. They predicted that, with the use of the word *good* by an interviewer in an attitude survey conducted by telephone, the interviewees' statements would be altered. During one half of the calls made, the interviewer answered, "good," after all responses by the interviewee that agreed with the survey statements; in the remaining calls, the interviewer answered, "good," only to dissenting responses. There was a significant difference between the two groups of interviewees: Those reinforced for agreeing became more agreeable, while those reinforced for disagreeing increased their disagreement.[5] The lesson is clear:

> When you reinforce acceptable or exceptional behavior by verbal recognition, you serve to extend such behavior and produce *more* acceptable or exceptional behavior.

Human values are at the core of efforts to obtain excellence from your subordinates. As a manager, you must be genuinely interested in the people who perform the work in your department. Displaying interest and obtaining positive results can be institutionalized in a plan for excellence. The plan would include the following elements:[6]

- Getting your people to see the end results of purposeful, consistent effort on their parts, as they relate to the advancement of their own careers
- Showing your subordinates how they fit into institutional goals; giving them deserved praise and meaningful recognition
- Giving the workers in your department an opportunity to achieve, recognizing that achievement in itself is a great motivator
- Knowing what your subordinates' personal goals are, and tying these in with the goals of the institution
- Helping your employees to set and achieve self-improvement goals
- Providing public acknowledgment of the accomplishments of your subordinates, to satisfy the key need for recognition and for feeling important
- Being continuously sensitive to the need to have your employees believe that they are accepted and approved by the institution and by their bosses
- Showing your employees how and why they are doing useful work
- Communicating to your subordinates about their progress
- Listening with interest to your subordinates' problems, their ideas, and their grievances
- Never neglecting, ignoring, or forgetting your subordinates

Here are five lessons to be learned from our discussion of the "Cornucopia of Fruit":[7]

1. Behavior that is rewarded will be reinforced and, therefore, more likely to be repeated.
2. Recognition and reinforcement should come as quickly as possible after the relevant performance or behavior is observed.
3. Subordinates crave recognition from their supervisors.
4. The recognition should fit the achievement.
5. Behavior you approve of and want should be rewarded; behavior you do not want should not be rewarded.

NOTES

1. Labor Relations Institute, *Foreman Facts* vol. 9, no. 21 (1970), 70.

2. Kenneth A. Kovach, "Why Motivational Theories Don't Work," *Advanced Management Journal,* Spring 1980: 71.

3. Theodore W. Kessler, "Management by Objectives," in *Handbook of Health Care Human Resources Management,* ed. Norman Metzger (Rockville, Md.: Aspen Systems Corporation, 1981), 184–186.

4. Willard Z. Merrihue, *Managing by Communication* (New York: McGraw Hill, 1960), 120.

5. Arnold P. Goldstein and Melvin Sorcher, *Changing Supervisor Behavior* (Newark, N.J.: Pergamon Press, 1974), 53–54.

6. Addison C. Bennett, "Effective Management Centers on Human Values," *Hospitals, JAHA,* 16 July 1976: 73–75.

7. For an excellent discussion of reinforcement, see Thomas L. Quick, *Understanding People at Work* (New York: Executive Enterprises Publications, 1970).

Chapter 4

Influencers: Controlling Others Who Control Others (Who Control Others)

THERE IS SOMETIMES CONSIDERABLE DIFFERENCE BETWEEN ELECTING SOMEONE TO BE PRESIDENT OF THE CLASS AND RECOGNIZING BY BALLOT SOMEONE WHO IS ALREADY LEADING THE CLASS. GROUPS WILL ALWAYS HAVE LEADERS. WHETHER OR NOT THOSE LEADERS WILL OCCUPY THE OFFICIAL LEADERSHIP POSITIONS IS ANOTHER QUESTION.

Robert M. Fulmer

4

Who really has the power to decide whether you or your organization will succeed or fail? Who really "calls the shots"? Usually, the "who's" are *not* the supervisors, *not* the department managers, *not* the medical and dental staff, perhaps *not* even top management. And yet, knowing the "who" is the key to extending your sphere of influence and gaining control of your own destiny.

Proof: Jimmy Carter did not have the answer and was destined to fail in his effort to gain the cooperation of other world leaders; he also had no chance of reelection. In contrast, Lyndon Johnson was able to accomplish in three months what John F. Kennedy could not achieve in three years; knowing the answer helped Johnson see the writing on the wall and choose not to run for reelection. Indeed, for all of us, knowing the answer can explain why those who themselves may not be too clever, innovative, or blessed with special talent can still develop enviable reputations as leaders.

WHO ARE THE INFLUENCERS?

In every group of people there will be someone who spontaneously is able to take charge—someone to whom, for unclear reasons, others look for guidance. No one elects them; in fact, sometimes their credentials seem unimpressive.

THESE ARE THE EGO-PEOPLE

The influencers—sometimes called informal leaders— are the people you must win over to your side. Jimmy Carter did not, and he failed. Lyndon Johnson did, and he

---

38

succeeded. Then he lost his followers, and he had to acknowledge failure. John F. Kennedy was partly successful, and his record reflects it. Many not-too-clever, not-too-innovative, not particularly talented men and women who rise to important leadership positions owe their success to the support of those with influence. These people are the *influencers*.

Learn to identify and win over the influencers, and you will achieve personal leadership success.

There are numerous practical advantages to be gained from identifying the influencers. For example, a negotiator who must get union agreement will succeed if those in leadership positions on the negotiating committee and among the rank-and-file believe the agreement should be accepted. A hospital president who needs board or medical staff support to provide a new program or service will succeed if the influencers on the board or among the physicians give their support. A newly appointed supervisor will be accepted and succeed if the influencers in the institution so decide. A parent who wants a child to be home on time will get obedience if the influencers in the child's social group have respect for the parent and want the parent's approval. Indeed, even the police have been successful in taming some street gangs after winning over the gang's leaders and enabling them to gain a more positive position in the community.

The quality of influence is complex, and perhaps indefinable, but the phenomenon exists. In a large family, there is probably one sibling (not always the male, nor the eldest) who somehow is able to "call the shots" for the others. Similarly, in social, religious, or community activities, there are usually one or two people to whom others turn for direction when problems arise. But why those particular people?

To make the issue even more complex, an individual who is acknowledged as the influencer in one setting may not have the same power in another. The brother who provides leadership within the home may learn that no one listens to him on the outside, while his sister who is ignored by the family may be a respected community leader, sought after for her counsel.

Whatever the reasons, whatever the causes, managers who want to survive during troubled times must depend on the influencers within their institution who will support their efforts, standards, and goals. Many health care CEOs succeed only to the extent the influencers on the board or on the medical staff permit. Getting the support of relevant influencers enables a manager to control employees, even those working in remote locations or on different shifts. And, when the manager's span of control grows to unmanageable proportions, the seemingly unwieldy group can be managed successfully if the manager ensures that the influencers within the workforce are supportive. Knowing that policies, procedures, and rules are being followed even during the manager's absence gives the manager control over the environment, and also peace of mind.

Influencers come in all shapes and sizes. At first glance, they may not look any different from anyone else. But there are tip-offs that reveal who they are. To spot the influencers:

- *Look for vocal people; identify those to whom people seem to listen.* Some call these people the "big mouths." They ask questions, have ideas, are filled with suggestions, speak up at meetings, talk to everybody. In an aimless meeting, invariably one person verbalizes what everybody is thinking: "We're going nowhere; there's got to be someone to take charge." (PS: They usually are asked to do so.) But be careful! There is a difference between the "big mouth" and the "loud mouth." People who make a lot of noise are deceptive; it is only when others listen to them that you have the genuine influencer.

- *Watch for the persons who seek out others.* They go to those in trouble or who have problems; they greet the visitor or the stranger; they notice when a fellow worker appears out of sorts; they tend to go where the action is, or will be. When new employees come aboard, an influencer usually suggests they join the others for coffee, lunch, or for a drink after work. And the new employee will not be accepted unless the influencer signals acceptance.

- *Identify people that others seek out.* Ask yourself, to whom do you turn when you have a problem (or a joy) that you feel has to be shared? Note to whom employees, and maybe even top management, turn when there is a crisis. Most groups have members who know whom to call for action or resolution of a problem. Successful politicians and community leaders know how important are the key people from whom they seek counsel when matters get tense or unpredictable. Even in families, there frequently is a particular relative or friend who is sought out in times of difficulty.

- *Watch for trend setters.* Frequently, one person in a group is the style and pace setter. That person may well be providing the leadership too. As a general rule, people tend to imitate those whom they respect (though may not always like). Thus you can identify the influencer by observing whom others imitate.

- *Look for those who represent the consensus.* While professing "not to speak for others," these people usually seem to reflect the opinions and values of others around them. They seem to speak to the responsive chord of a group.

- *Identify those who set work standards.* Many an industrial engineer has been mistrusted in efforts to improve worker efficiency because of a conflict with an influencer. Regardless of what the engineer has determined *should* be the work standard, the influencer usually has the last word. (Likewise, efforts to improve efficiency succeed, not necessarily because of the proper design of work flow, but because those who are the influencers are willing to adopt the new standards.)

- *Look for those who have a "spark."* Whatever other evidence exists, a single characteristic seems to epitomize the influencer: each influencer radiates (though sometimes quietly) a spark—a charisma. The spark, unfortunately, is not always positive; indeed, a turned-off influencer may seem abrasive and negative and may just set off sparks rather than be sparkling. But positive or negative, influencers possess a quality that sets them off from their peers, and this quality *must* be recognized.

HOW DO YOU WIN OVER INFLUENCERS?

Identifying the influencer is the first step toward gaining control and acceptance. It provides a basis for the design of strategy and can enable you to take action. Next, to win over influencers, you must take some additional steps.

First, ask for advice. There are few things more flattering to influencers than to have someone in authority or leadership ask for their advice. The request for advice says, "I respect you." It lets influencers know that they are important somebodys in the eyes of others. (It also might mean that the influencers will support your actions since you have been wise enough to seek their counsel.)

It is important to remember that the act of seeking advice does not obligate you to take it. It is mandatory, though, that you avoid appearing as if you are manipulating the influencer. Seek advice only if you might follow that advice. And always acknowledge the advice and the adviser.

There are two times when the advice of an influencer can be safely sought:

1. When you truly are uncertain as to what direction you want to take or what decision to make. At such times, the advice of the influencer might be just what is needed.
2. When there are several alternatives, all of which are acceptable to you. At such time, allowing the influencer to give advice as to the "better" alternative will ensure that both of you are satisfied.

Second, ask for an opinion. There are times and circumstances when seeking advice is just not appropriate or practical. If the social relationship or organizational status inhibits you, a "safer" way to win over the influencer is to request an opinion. Seeking an opinion is safer than asking outright for advice, but it still is flattering, and it demonstrates your respect for the influencer.

Seeking an opinion is also safer because the degree of obligation to adopt what has been suggested is lessened. Even better, the influencer is not on the spot since the opinion can be given in general terms and the influencer's responsibility is thereby lessened.

Also, seeking an opinion while showing that you respect the influencer's views provides sufficient leeway for the influencer to gracefully admit a lack of competence to offer a helpful opinion.

Third, give or share responsibility. Influencers, by definition, are leaders. You should recognize this fact and give them responsibilities in areas in which they believe they are competent. This will ensure that the influencers give it their very best shot, and they will also feel good about you.

Of course, difficulties can arise if there is a difference of opinion between you and the influencer as to the influencer's level of competence. The influencer may seek more responsibility than you want to give. Unless this issue is addressed, the outcome of extending the responsibility may be negative rather than positive. (One answer to this dilemma—a sound, practical, and effective one—is provided in the following chapter.)

In any case, allowing the influencer to enjoy greater responsibility is a formidable tool. It is a visible way of communicating confidence in and respect for the influencer. It also allows you to move on to other tasks.

Beware, however—the giving or sharing of responsibilities requires some risk taking. If you're the type who must do everything yourself and you have trouble trusting others, you probably won't survive in troubled times (unless you are independently wealthy and do not depend upon your job to survive). To prosper, you will need to learn low-risk ways to work with and through influencers, despite the risks involved in seeking advice and opinions. For example, if you assign responsibility to a certain person, that person may not succeed. Still, the risks can be minimized if you use the tools of requesting advice or an opinion only when there is little potential for severe damage or harm. Above all, be careful not to ask for help on matters in which failure or error is unacceptable.

Fourth, keep the influencers "in on things." When people are under stress or anxious, one potent remedy is to keep them in-the-know about what is happening and what is being planned. When we believe we know what is going on about us, we develop a brighter perspective, and our feelings about those who give us information are positive. We are complimented when a boss or other VIP spends time and effort to communicate with us. It shows they care about our feelings and are aware of our place on the team.

Of course, it is desirable to keep everyone up to date. But it's *vital* to keep influencers fully aware on matters of interest to them.

When influencers are left out of the information-sharing process, their power can become particularly evident in negative ways. The key is to use their influence to lead others for the greater good of the group.

A hospital departmental manager was worried about a census drop that threatened the institution. The workers were bitter. They believed the hospital was exaggerating while it exploited them. So without revealing specific figures, the manager shared with the influencers the financial status of the institution. His willingness to share this information bolstered his credibility, and the influencers convinced others that things were not as good as they believed. As census improved, these key influencers were kept current. Thus, nonmanagement employees helped significantly to improve the efficiency and effectiveness of the institution. They accepted the figures, and trust was established. Oh yes, the manager made certain that the employees shared in the improved operating picture, and their rewards were real.

Many health care managers have found that discharging an employee goes more smoothly when certain influencers are informed—properly and ethically—in advance. The often-heard claim that "the person deserved to be fired, but the way it was done was unpardonable," can be prevented if you ensure that the relevant influencers have sufficient advance information to prevent the potential backlash.

Fifth, match motive and reward. If you are going to thrive in today's hectic competitive health care world, you must ensure that those who call the shots feel good about you and what you are doing. To do this, you must use a system of rewards keyed to motivation. You can motivate influencers and other employees by meeting their needs. Influencers have a need to be acknowledged as leaders. If you demonstrate your recognition of and respect for them as leaders through visible rewards, you will benefit from their support as you work toward your goals.

Regardless of the locale—in Congress, in the family, in the administrative office, or in the board room—if the influencers find their needs are met because of their association with you, they will be more apt to respond the way you want. And even when they disagree, their disagreement will be without the hostility and rancor that comes from an adversarial relationship.

A word of caution: When you form your partnership with influencers, you will have formed a team. But a team means a bit less independence for you. At first you may feel you are giving up a piece of your flesh in return for a bit of shared power. But it is worth it! In truth, your power will increase and your leadership will be enhanced as others share your values and support you, as you move ever closer to your goals.

Chapter 5

It's Not a Question of Who's Talking, but of Who's Listening

IN EFFECT, THE SELF ORIENTED CHARACTER SAYS: "I CAN CONTRIBUTE MORE, IF THEY LISTEN TO MY IDEAS, IF I AM TREATED AS AN INDIVIDUAL, NEITHER AS A CHILD NOR A MACHINE, AND THE REWARDS ARE FAIR. OTHERWISE, I'LL LOOK OUT FOR MYSELF."

Michael Maccoby

5

If there is one area where the modern health care leader usually fails, it is in communication. Yet communication is the most valuable tool that modern business has to reach agreement on institutional objectives and to direct efforts toward achieving those objectives.

In a study by the American Management Associations of superior-subordinate communication at the managerial level, researchers found that,

> if a single answer can be drawn from this detailed research study, . . . it is this: if one is speaking of the subordinate's specific job—his duties, the requirements he must fulfill in order to do his work well, his intelligent anticipation of future changes in his work, and the obstacles which prevent him from doing as good a job as possible—he and his boss do not agree, or differ more than they agree, in almost every area.[1]

Over the years, we have wasted energy and economic resources by concentrating on the *form* of communication rather than its *substance*. In effect, we have engaged in the counterproductive habit of seeking directions when motoring in areas not familiar to us, stopping at gas stations or hailing a pedestrian or another driver, and then riding away without having absorbed the advice or instructions. We left without the capacity to remember, for the simple reason that *we were not listening*.

Half the process of communication is listening—not just sitting *back* and listening, but sitting *up* and listening. The old cliche, "what we have here is a failure to communicate," can be paraphrased more realistically and accurately: "What we have here is the result of poor listening habits."

HOW TO IMPROVE YOUR LISTENING

The better listener a manager is, the better listening the manager will inspire. Here are some tips on improving your listening habits that you can pass on to your co-workers:

First, most of us talk too much. We spend too much time explaining our own positions at the expense of understanding where the other person stands.

TRY THIS

Use judicious silence. At the beginning of a discussion, confine yourself to asking questions and then remaining silent for a period of time after each question is proffered.

Silence is a great motivator to get the other person to speak up. The best way to gauge your own listening capacity is to time your own periods of silence.

Second, most of us frame questions to get the answers we *want* to hear, so

---

TRY THIS

Use open-ended questions. Frame your questions so that you leave the way open for whatever type of answer the other person truly wants to give, and let the other person finish answering. Then at the point you initially think the person has finished, just grunt a little, nod a little, and let the person continue, just in case—and more often than not it *is* the case—the person has something more to say.

Third, most of us set up communication in a counterproductive atmosphere.

TRY THIS

Schedule discussions regarding problems when the facts and details are fresh in everyone's mind. Pick a time and place that provide maximum comfort. If the situation is emotion-laden, "take ten"—provide for a cooling-off period. Most importantly, ensure that you protect the dignity of all parties in the communication process.

Fourth, much communication is done on an ad hoc basis with little preparation or fact-finding.

TRY THIS

Save yourself a lot of time and aggravation by checking records and investigating facts ahead of time. It might be helpful to request a detailed report from your subordinate in advance of a meeting between you and the subordinate. The report can serve as a point of departure for the discussion.

Finally, many of us let emotion-laden filters get in the way of understanding.

TRY THIS

Listen for *feelings*. Pay attention to the way other persons say things as well as to what they say. Pay attention to the way you say something as well as to what you say. A good way to perfect your listening for feelings is deliberately to put aside the facts and details of the presentation, dig deeply, and listen to the *overall* approach. You can then check out what you sense with these phrases: "I conclude that you approve (or disapprove) of . . .;" or, "Am I right in concluding that what you are saying is. . . ."

THE ART OF COMMUNICATION

Communication is the prime tool of the modern manager, and probably also the most difficult one to perfect. What complicates the whole communications structure is that there are so many different messages involved. It has been suggested that each communication involves at least six messages:

1. What you *mean* to say
2. What you *actually* say
3. What the other person *hears*
4. What the other person *thinks* he or she hears

5. What the other person *says*
6. What you *think* the other person says

How do you attempt to overcome these hurdles? Here's a suggestion: The next time you are in a discussion, a debate, or an argument, invoke this rule: Before you reply to the other person's comments, *repeat* what the other person has said. Before the person replies to your comment, have the person repeat what you have said. Believe us when we say that this exercise will be both an eye and an ear opener!

Are You a Good Listener?

A simplistic view of communication focuses on *talking*. There is of course also the simplistic focus on memo writing. In both cases, this archaic view paints a picture of a lone communicator in an empty room. Reality would introduce into that room another person—someone who is listening. Half the process of communication is listening—not idle reception, but an active performance in which the listener sits up and exerts, both physically and mentally in order to understand.

> Communication is a joint effort: someone talks and someone listens—not just sitting *back* and listening, but sitting *up* and listening.

It is clear that the better listener a manager is, the better listening the manager will inspire. Too often, people tend to hear what they want to hear and to close their ears to what they do not want to hear. Yet one can never communicate in a vacuum. Effective communication flows from sound employee relations.

> If you are to obtain honest and objective communication *from* your subordinates, they must believe that that is exactly what you are doing *with* them. They come to that belief by looking at the history of their relationship with you. Specifically, has what you've told them in the past been accurate, open, and factual? Can they rely on your word?

If your subordinates believe that you do not play favorites, that you do not hog all the credit or pass the buck, that you back them up, and that you are fair and dependable, they will listen to what you have to say.

How To Guarantee Effective Communication

Research indicates that managers who hope to meet universal standards for effective communication with their employees must take the following four steps:[2]

1. Gain the confidence of their employees by:

   • being impartial and consistent

   • making no commitments they cannot fulfill

   • making certain that all problems and grievances are answered properly and correctly

   • making the employees' work problems their own—and actively representing their employees' interests at other levels of management

   • making it clear that the institution has grievance machinery that works.

2. Gain the respect and friendship of their employees by:

   • according respectful treatment to each employee as an individual and esteemed associate, showing sincere interest in the person's welfare

   • displaying enthusiasm about their progress

   • being considerate and helpful in all possible ways

   • demonstrating sincere personal interest in matters that are important from the employees' point of view.

3. In the receptive climate thus established (with good downward communication to receptive employees and good upward communication from employees who feel free to discuss matters with the manager), skills must be developed such as:

   • listening

   • talking

   • selling

4. Most important is the ability to listen carefully in order to achieve full understanding of the information received, to take action quickly based on this understanding, and to communicate the results of such action to the individuals involved.

Six Soul-Searching Questions for Effective Communication

Ask yourself these six questions before you attempt to communicate with your employees:[3]

1. Do I assume that if an idea is clear to me that it will be clear to the receiver? (Not necessarily so.)
2. Do I make it comfortable for others to tell me what is really on their minds, or do I encourage them to tell me only what I would like to hear? (It had better be the former.)
3. Do I check my understanding of what another person has told me before I reply? (Feedback is essential to effective communication.)
4. Am I tolerant of other people's feelings, realizing that their feelings, which may be different from mine, affect their communication? (We are always dealing with human emotions.)
5. Do I really try to listen from the sender's point of view before evaluating the message from my point of view? (There are two people in most conversations; the other person has a point of view.)
6. Do I make a conscious effort to build a feedback possibility in all communications, since even at its best communication is an imperfect process? (Does the other person hear what I meant to say?)

CONCLUSION

People who participate in the shaping of change are more likely to be receptive to the change and, therefore, more productive. Increased participation in decision making can be an effective management tool, depending on the management style that has preceded it. If your subordinates believe that you truly value their ideas, that you will consider their suggestions objectively, that they can be free to voice their concerns to you—then, and only then, will their participation be effective. Such an atmosphere facilitates good communication.

Although effective communication requires an expert use of media, the greatest barrier to communication probably lies in the area of human relations. People must trust you in order to hear you and, of course, then to believe you. Half the process of communication is listening. The better listener the supervisor is, the better listening the supervisor will inspire.

No matter what form the communication takes, there is always a sender and there is always a receiver. The sender needs a receiver who will tune into the message and clear up the static. Keep in mind that effective communication springs from an atmosphere, from an environment, that encourages rather than discourages trust. We fail in communication when there is fear or suspicion. We fail when we view the listener as invisible.

With the advent of large institutions and complex employee relations problems, modern managers, although ennobled by techniques and methods far superior to their predecessors, have paid a high price for "overspecialization." We are pressed to get things done at the cost of achieving understanding. To the extent that we develop and refine the art of communicating, to that extent we will be effective managers.

Your skill as a communicator is essential to your success as a manager and to the productivity of your subordinates. Productivity stems from an understanding of goals and of the process needed to obtain them. This understanding is dependent upon your skill as a communicator. No matter how varied your activities—how important your responsibilities may be and how specialized your other skills are—in the final analysis your success as a manager is related to communication.

Beware of the "nodders." They are the people who keep nodding as if they understand. Also beware of those who are very protective as to their own positions and thus pay lip service to you to minimize the chances of your being vindictive or unhappy. If you want to avoid these types and build commitment, you must set up an environment wherein a free flow and exchange of information, up and down the line, are possible. Still other persons may hear only what they want to hear and close their ears to what they do not want to hear. This may well be a reflection of their past relationships with you.

If you are to obtain honest objective communication with your subordinates, they must believe that you are operating with honesty and objectivity. If you have been fair in the past, if you have shared credit in the past, if you have backed them up in the past, they will listen to what you have to say. The greatest barrier to communication is in the area of human relations. If you want people to listen, treat them like human beings. It's as simple as that.

NOTES

1. Norman R.F. Maier, L. Richard Hoffman, John J. Hooven, and William H. Read, *Superior-Subordinate Communication in Management*, AMA Research Study 52 (New York: American Management Associations, 1961), 9.

2. Willard B. Merrihue, *Managing by Communication* (New York: McGraw Hill, 1960), 108–109.

3. Norman Metzger, *The Health Care Supervisor's Handbook*, 2nd ed. (Rockville, Md.: Aspen Systems Corporation, 1982), 70.

Chapter 6

Delegation Updated: Please Mom, I Can Do It Myself

ANDREW CARNEGIE ONCE REMARKED THAT WHEN A MAN REALIZES HE CAN CALL OTHERS IN TO HELP HIM DO A BETTER JOB THAN HE CAN DO ALONE, HE HAS TAKEN A BIG STEP IN LIFE. IN LIKE MANNER, TEDDY ROOSEVELT OBSERVED THAT THE BEST EXECUTIVE IS THE ONE WHO HAS SENSE ENOUGH TO PICK GOOD MEN TO DO WHAT HE WANTS DONE AND SELF-RESTRAINT ENOUGH TO KEEP FROM MEDDLING WITH THEM WHILE THEY DO IT.

James J. Cribbin

6

During these troubled times, when stress and strain are increasing on most health care managers, the ability to apply communication skills tends to diminish. We lose patience, our messages are cryptic; too frequently we take things for granted instead of pursuing doubts about them. The cliche, "I can do it myself faster than I can teach someone else" becomes the operative credo. Under pressure, too many managers quickly become unwilling to trust another person to carry out an assignment; they become unwilling to take risks.

Much has been said about the "art and science" of delegation. Delegation is usually said to need elaborate formulas and techniques. However, delegation need not be so complicated. Without being simplistic, you can use a single approach most of the time. This approach makes sense, is conceptually easy to understand, is readily communicated to others; and, it works!

THE COMMUNICATION APPROACH

The trouble with most approaches to delegation is that they are "scientific," they are planned rationally and intellectually. Yet delegation is really an emotional process, not a scientific one. Scientific "human relations" ingredients are absent, because, when we delegate, we are handing over to another person responsibility for our responsibilities.

Moreover, most of us find that, when we are under pressure, we have little patience with rational, intellectual concepts and theories. What we need is an approach to handle the emotional side of delegation—an approach that is as much a communication tool as it is a managerial device. To test this communication approach to delegation, consider the following five typical human management dilemmas:

1. A competent worker thinks more highly of himself than you do. He is reaching out for responsibility, but you have low confidence in him and do not want to risk failure. (You are damned if you do and damned if you don't!)
2. You are not sure whether an individual has the correct answer to a problem or is capable of making a particular decision. You are not sure how you can be certain that this is the time to take a risk. (You are damned if you do and damned if you don't!)
3. An employee lacks confidence and is timid about her ability to carry out an assignment. Forcing her to do it because "you have faith in her" may be counterproductive. If she fails, she will be further demoralized. Because of her current state of mind, she is dooming herself to failure. (You're damned if you do and damned if you don't!)
4. There are two people with similar jobs, but your confidence in one is greater than in the other. You are faced with a charge of favoritism. If you refuse to give the person in whom you have less confidence an opportunity, you might be hurting yourself as well as that person. (You're damned if you do and damned if you don't!)
5. You want to "stretch" someone but are concerned about whether you're moving her along too quickly. You fear holding the individual back, yet you're not certain whether she is able to assume greater responsibility. (You're damned if you do and damned if you don't!)

At least one of these dilemmas is probably all too familiar to you. You *are* damned if you do and damned if you don't, unless you use solid communication and managerial skills to decrease risks for both you and your employees.

To make certain that you can delegate effectively, there must be absolute clarity as to the amount of authority involved. All parties involved must know how much "freedom" the individual to whom responsibility is being delegated has to implement actions. Knowing the amount of freedom—the authority level—can reduce anxiety and help concentrate energies on the doing of the delegated tasks. Too many health care employees who are trained to make critical clinical decisions are frustrated by the belief that they have responsibility without sufficient authority.

THE FOX TROT TECHNIQUE

BE AWARE

Clarification of the extent of a person's authority should mirror your trust and that person's self-confidence. When the two elements blend, everyone has peace of mind. That's our objective. This approach may be called the "fox trot" technique.

The term *fox trot* honors (with only some tongue in cheek) those who believe delegation is a management "dance." It is in fact a three-move approach, thus the term may make it easier to remember and use it. (Incidentally, follow-up action is vital to make certain that the person to whom you have delegated responsibility does what it is you wanted done and achieves the results that you have identified. How to do this is covered in another chapter.)

The Three-Step Moves

The correct level of authority to assign in any given circumstances will reflect the amount of trust you have in the person. The authority level also needs to be in tune with the person's degree of self-confidence. At each level of authority, a managerial move communicates a different message.

TELL THE DELEGATEE

Move 1—(You're on your own) Do it! I need not know the "whats," "hows," or "whys."

Move 2—(Keep me posted) Do it, *but* be sure to tell me the what and how and why *after* you've done it.

Move 3—(Check it out) Decide! Determine what you want to do and how you want to do it, but tell me *before* you proceed.

A side comment on Move 3: It's an excellent way to determine whether a decision has been thoroughly thought out and whether the recommended actions meet your criteria. Also, it can help you learn more about the individual's abilities.

Here are some guidelines for applying the fox trot technique, using the above moves:

- Move 1: For situations in which a person has been keeping you involved unnecessarily or in which your trust and confidence is high. Move 1 should be used with individuals who have the know-how but are unsure about the amount of authority they have. They may have been delaying action, or they may habitually prepare reports and feedback to you, thus avoiding action because of history, ritual, caution, or fear.
- Move 2: For situations in which you have to know what is taking place—when you are accountable for an action, or when your position requires you

to be kept informed and up to date. Move 2 should be used when your confidence in a person is low and you want to verify results. You will find it useful as a strategy to develop new or untried workers. Obviously, it should be used only when, if something goes awry, the negative results are not irreparable. This move can be a powerful tool for insecure or frightened employees, for example, when you have a great deal more trust in your employees than they have in themselves. The reporting to you gives them "freedom" while providing them with the comfort that they will get immediate feedback or support and will not have to face being left alone, hoping everything was satisfactory.

- Move 3: For situations in which you are unsure or have a low level of trust and confidence in someone. Move 3 will give you a chance to evaluate the person's thought processes and plans before any action is undertaken. This move not only provides confidence that actions being taken meet with your approval, it also enables you to keep a tight rein on any informal leaders who have greater confidence in their ability than you have. Move 3 is effective with new employees who need to be tested, for example, with newly graduated nurses, technologists, or therapists. It also provides an opportunity to assess the development and growth of employees who may be seeking greater challenges in their jobs and careers.

CAUTION! DELEGATION MEANS TAKING RISKS

Delegate only when you are willing to allow an employee to fail (although the employee usually will succeed). Delegate only in situations that will not bring the proverbial walls crashing down if your plans do not work out. Also, remember that with Move 3, though you do not have to accept every decision, you do need to explain why the recommendation was rejected, thereby reaffirming your respect for the individual.

Like most other management tools, the fox trot technique works in personal life as well. Assigning Moves 1, 2, or 3 to a child is an excellent way to develop the child's self-confidence and to determine whether the child is ready for greater independence and freedom. Move 3 works as well with physical tasks; the child can describe how the task will be done or perhaps give a short demonstration of what should be done and how.

By the way, if workers (or a child) want less authority than you're prepared to give, go along with them. Let them develop confidence before you insist they take on greater responsibility and authority.

Some Safeguards

Okay, you've learned the fox trot technique. And you can apply it. But you are not through yet. What happens when you are not sure about the amount of authority you want to delegate? Or what do you do if you find yourself the one to whom something is delegated and your boss does not know the technique? You are in a quandary again—how much authority do you have? Worry, worry, worry. Well, in such situations you can play games and conveniently ''forget'' to use the technique (thus leaving the person with anxiety and doubt and giving yourself an ''out'' if things don't work out satisfactorily). Or you can use some safeguards.

TRY THIS

If you are unsure of how much authority you wish to delegate:

- Train your employees in the fox trot technique so that they know the rules and can question you if you have not been clear. Go a step further: Train them to tell you how much authority they are taking or wish to take when you do not clarify their authority. You can then react to their suggestions.
- Even if the decision or action does not work out as planned, everyone involved at least has peace of mind and a shared understanding of the amount of freedom to act that was authorized. Obviously, if a person is planning to exercise greater authority than you are comfortable with, you will then have a chance to react immediately rather than wait until it is too late. The clarity inherent in this style of communication can benefit everyone.

AND TRY THIS

If you are not sure how much authority you have or you are unclear as to the amount of freedom to act you possess, let your boss know how much authority you are planning to take. You'll get a reaction if your are reaching out too far. If you are not successful in your assignment, you will at least have eliminated the anxiety that comes with "not knowing how far to go."

The fox trot technique is not always foolproof. People do play many games. However, it is an excellent communication device, a tried and proven way of reducing anxiety, and a quick and effective way of getting things done, with peace of mind.

Chapter 7

"Monkey Training": Getting Others To Follow Your Style, Your Example, Your Behavior—and Your Direction

IF MANAGERS ARE CARELESS ABOUT BASIC THINGS—TELLING THE TRUTH, RESPECTING MORAL CODES, PROPER PROFESSIONAL CONDUCT—WHO CAN BELIEVE THEM ON OTHER ISSUES?

James L. Hayes

7

"You can't teach an old dog new tricks." Bunk! "You can't change those who are set in their ways." Not true! "People who are negative are negative about everything." False!

With the use of a simple concept, you have the power to change the attitudes and behaviors of those with whom you must work and live. Though a bit of concentration and effort (and practice) is needed, there are no special talents or tricks involved. You will be using some basic and natural physiological and psychological principles that you've been using all along, but *without controlling them*. An understanding of this approach will give you control. It will enable you to use this leadership tool immediately, and to enjoy dividends almost as quickly.

As your doubt and cynicism are replaced by success, you will have increased power to instill a positive attitude in what may have been dispirited employees. You will be able to reduce the number of errors made by others, and possibly also to get others to learn better and faster.

APPLIED MIMICRY: THE IMPACT OF ENVIRONMENT

> From the time you are born, you are learning—you are learning words, values, behavior. As we grow, we "ape" our friends, our parents, our teachers, and others with whom we come in contact. We are not consciously aware of how much we are learning, but our senses are pulling in and storing information, ranging from the meanings of words to how to behave in certain situations. We pick up values and learn how to behave. We mimic, we ape, we copy, and we believe.

> Understanding how we become what we are enables us to influence how others will be. This is power!

Behavioral scientists are far from agreement on how much our behavior is affected by environmental versus hereditary factors. The more they argue, however, the more they acknowledge the very powerful influence of environment. Without getting into a psychological morass, it is clear we speak a language because it is the one to which we have been exposed. We develop the customs of our society because we are immersed in that society. And certainly, while we are able to think and develop new values later in life, we still are influenced tremendously by our earliest exposures.

In fact, we are influenced daily by our environment. When we walk into a room filled with laughing people, we join the merriment—we are swept up into it. The behavior is infectious, and it is difficult to resist. Conversely, when a boss (or a spouse) is angry or depressed, we frequently get trapped by that person's moods. The negativism permeates us, and we adopt the person's sullenness. Similarly, the mood of a surgeon can influence the attitude of every employee in an OR.

Of course, we are also influenced by our past. The roots of someone's peppy disposition are to be found in that person's parents or teachers. A parent may have taught the person that bright and optimistic behavior is "normal." Thus, our behavior clearly owes much to our past.

Here's another example: A friend is an indefatigable optimist. Everything is positive, everything is good. It is difficult to be negative in her presence; she does not let you get away with it. Then we are introduced to this friend's small son, who, probably without knowing what he is saying, greets us with a little hand, a big smile, and a "God bless you—I love you—have a nice day!" The connection is obvious!

Monkey Training

TRY THIS

1. Place on a piece of paper the names of those who have been closest to you during your life, including your closest friends.
2. Note to yourself how each person on the list expresses joy, anger, displeasure; how each reacts to disappointments, frustration, success.
3. Match your behavior with that of each person on the list. You will see just how well you have picked up patterns of behavior from your "teachers."

> 4. Continue: See how many people you can identify in your life from whom you have learned a value, a behavior, or a belief. You are the composite of many—some more than others.

The power gained from understanding and using this concept will enable you to control much of the behavior of those around you. We are human, but the old proverb "Monkey see, monkey do," describes much of our behavior.

Caution: Habits are habitforming. Before rushing off to apply monkey training, recognize that, when we learn behavior or ideas so thoroughly that they become unconscious, we call them habits. Habits can be changed; but, when a behavior or belief has been reinforced over a long period of time, it is like a block of concrete that is not easily moved. Thus monkey training works, but you need patience.

Recognize that patterns developed over a long period of time become ingrained and govern our thinking and actions without our being consciously aware of them. For example, have you ever driven to work but later could not recall having done so? We dress in the morning, we brush our teeth, we go through hundreds of mundane, simple exercises each day without the slightest bit of concentration. In fact, we are good at doing many things so automatically that we find it difficult to teach those things to others.

TRY THIS TEST

1. Teach someone to tie a shoelace *without* first doing it yourself.
2. Slowly recite the words of the "Star Spangled Banner" without first singing or humming the tune, even mentally.
3. Fill in the blanks for the following associations:

   • French men make _____lovers.
   • Blondes have more _____.
   • The good guys always wear _____hats.

Simply put, if you want to influence the behavior and attitude of those around you, demonstrate the desired behavior or attitude. Maintain the behavior or attitude whenever you are in their presence, and observe how it becomes contagious. As a manager—or a parent—practice specific ways of doing things when teaching others, and watch as you are "aped." Hold a tool in a certain position, carry out a certain work procedure—and watch them mimic you.

TRY THIS

1. Walk into a room of workers (or family members) with a broad smile. Observe the facial expressions of those present.
2. Suddenly change your smile to a deep frown. Observe how the lines of their mouths turn down and their moods change to reflect yours.
3. Observe how those closest to you, on or off the job, practice habits they have seen in you.

Thus, ideas, habits, and values can be changed. Today, we are always looking for a quick fix and an immediate payoff; monkey training will produce plenty of quick fixes and quick payoffs. But if you are seeking to change deep-rooted habits or beliefs, be patient. The greater the conviction, the more ingrained the habit, the more patience you will need before others respond.

Positive Monkeys vs. Negative Monkeys

If it's true—and it is—that we mimic others, that we learn much through observation and mimicry, it stands to reason that if we are taught only positives, we, in turn, will become more positive; if we are taught only the right way of doing something, we will be more apt to learn only the right way to do it.

Unfortunately, our brains and consciences, though powerful, are also frail. Frequently, we fail to see, hear, or interpret properly. Frequently, we cannot distinguish between messages of different qualities, and thus we misconstrue directions. For example, the employee who has a poor supervisor may vow never to practice the kind of management to which he has been subjected, only to find that, in the same situation, he practices the rejected management behavior. Similarly, mothers who abuse their children tend to be those who have been abused as children; they are filled with remorse and "don't know why" they do it.

Moreover, we associate negative things with certain kinds of behavior. Phobias frequently are developed by associating events with negative emotions. Thus,

"I fell off a ladder."
"Ladders are dangerous."
"Ladders are high."
"High is dangerous."

ERGO

"Airplanes go high—they are dangerous."
"Elevators go high—they are dangerous."
Etc., etc., etc.—"I have acrophobia."

TEST YOURSELF

1. Think of a food you ate prior to getting a case of the flu
   or other stomach ailment. Do you still enjoy that food?
   As much as usual? If you do, how long did it take
   before you could go back to eating it after your ill-
   ness?
2. Think of a poor habit someone who is close to you
   practices regularly. In times of stress, have you ever
   copied that behavior, all the while knowing it was the
   wrong thing to do?
3. When you have been told about, and shown repeat-
   edly, something you have done wrong, do you find
   yourself still repeating the wrong behavior?
4. When someone enters a room, call out, "Don't look at
   me!" and see how they respond.

The difficulty with negative monkey training is that it's easy, it's habitual, and
it's all around us. We see street signs that say, "Don't Walk," elevator signs that
say, "In case of fire, use only stairs;" or we tell people, "Don't stare," "Stop
shouting," "Don't get nervous." Yet, in spite of all these admonitions, that's
exactly what the people do or become. What's the alternative?

POSITIVE MONKEY TRAINING

If we tell people only what it is we want them to do, and
avoid reinforcing negative behavior, it's possible that they
won't be able to perform the negative behavior, since it will
not have been learned. If, when we train employees, children, or others to do something, we exclude those things
that will lead to errors or bad behavior, it's conceivable that
they won't learn the improper technique or behavior.

Fact: If you know only the right way to do something, if
you know only what you are supposed to know, if you

witness only the correct behavior, the odds for achieving success are enhanced dramatically.

TRY THIS

1. When someone enters a room, cry out, "Look at the floor." Watch the person stare in the direction of the floor.
2. Change all the training manuals, guidebooks, and instructions within your sphere of authority; include only descriptions of what it is the reader is to do and learn, removing all negative or "don't-do" statements. Watch the results.
3. When people make an error or mistake, repeat (or even better, have *them* repeat) the proper way. If they ask what it was they did wrong, refuse to dwell on the negative side. Let them know why, and continue to work on the positive side. You'll see positive results.
4. When an employee, friend, or family member is under stress, suggest that the person relax—enjoy—rest—look at the bright side. Watch the visible change in the person.

When, during the Watergate crisis, Richard Nixon appeared before a world audience and said that "your president is not a crook," the White House was bombarded by thousands of telephone calls and telegrams from people who had not heard the words "is not" and were shocked that the president would say that "he was a crook." Our ears often don't function well; our minds are faulty organisms, our observations and attentiveness need work. Thus, we need the best odds possible!

THE PERSONAL ROLE MODEL: RISING TO THE TOP OF THE JUNGLE

Positive monkey training is a sophisticated tool that leads to bright horizons. It will help you become what you never thought you could be. It can change your own attitudes as well as those of people around you. It can help you shine in arenas that you might have avoided previously. It will help you become comfortable in unfamiliar surroundings. There is no mystery to the technique—just a requirement that you consistently *use* positive monkey training.

The Importance of Role Models

When professional actors perform new roles, solid research is a must. Obviously, today's actors cannot mimic from personal experience the behavior of French peasants during the Middle Ages. Yet when they are given such roles, they are expected to play them realistically. So they research their characters. They read. They study. They explore. They build models of the roles they will adopt so that they can immerse themselves in the characters they will portray. In the same way, nursing educators have, for many years, been using examples of clinical role models in the training of new nurses. Researching a role is crucial to positive monkey training.

Equally significant is the impact actors have upon us as they act out their roles. If they play their parts well, we react accordingly—we experience grief, we feel the fatigue of age, our spirits brighten. It is our nature to react to the behavior of others. Thus, if you thoroughly research the role you want for yourself and carry it out, you will be able to determine how others react to you. In other words, custom design your own role model, adopt characteristics of that role, and others will react to you accordingly.

Consider some examples of leadership at work. In 1932, when Franklin Delano Roosevelt stood before a world of depression and despair, there were only glimmers of hope. However, when he told the American public that "we have nothing to fear but fear itself," he rallied millions of people and bred confidence where there had been only despair. (Can you imagine the impact he would have had if he had expressed doubt and anxiety?) Roosevelt was demonstrating confidence and hope; he was being a role model for the American people.

Perhaps even more dramatically, when the great aerialist Karl Wallenda fell ten stories from a high wire to his death during an outdoor performance, his family members, also performers, looked on in horror. That night, they performed as usual: With the band playing and the crowd applauding, they smiled and took their bows. Their hearts might have been breaking, but they carried out their roles as professionals whose job was to make the public enjoy the performance. In the same manner, many an emergency room nurse must put on a pleasant face for a critically ill patient's family. As a professional, the nurse must mask all of the real emotions being experienced.

> Personal leadership may be difficult at times, but the reputation and respect you develop stimulates even greater efforts.

The Art of Role Modeling

You can use a role model to achieve almost anything. Let's say you are asked to make a speech before a large audience. You're frightened. You're not sure you should accept the assignment, even though it's a great opportunity.

YOU COULD TRY THIS

1. List those characteristics that you associate with successful, dynamic speakers (knowledgeable? at ease? sense of humor? modulated voice? enthusiastic?).
2. Conduct your "research" so that you are familiar with the role model you have designed for yourself. Familiarize yourself with the behavior of a successful, dynamic speaker.
3. Immerse yourself in your role. Act out each of the characteristics. If necessary, practice in front of a mirror or in front of a spouse or friend. Be thorough. Learn how to play the role of a successful, dynamic speaker.
4. Accept that you may be nervous, frightened, insecure, unhappy. So what? No one asked you to feel comfortable; nor do you have to be comfortable. (In fact, if you wait until you feel comfortable, you will never get to the speech.)
5. Imagine that you are on stage and about to start the presentation. Play the role in practice.
6. Carry out the role. No one will know how you feel inside. They'll just see a relaxed, enthusiastic speaker.

You can adopt a role to fit the circumstances of almost any moment. If you want to demonstrate a specific image, quickly assemble the relevant role model and immerse yourself mentally in it.

TRY THIS

Before being introduced to someone you are meeting for the first time, plan out a role model for yourself. Think

> through the role model's behavioral characteristics and act
> them out. Watch how your behavior influences the person's
> treatment of you.

Is this being artificial? Absolutely not. It's just one aspect of a sound personal leadership style. Indeed, the use of positive role modeling enables many people to succeed in spite of personal doubts. After many years on the stage, many actors have noted the tremendous stage fright and fear that still engulfs them before a performance. However, once on stage, when they are immersed in their roles, their performance is outstanding. In the same way, when you're "on stage," the manner in which you live up to your personal role model will be the measure of your personal success.

Role Modeling for Success

Now for the development of the ultimate personal role model. You want to move up and out. You want to reach levels that at the moment appear beyond you. You want to be respected in a way that you have not enjoyed before. Well, now it's time to look at your target role models. Many of us have heroes that we admire and try to emulate, but frequently our heroes cannot be emulated, and we are frustrated. In such cases, why not establish an imaginary role model against which you can judge yourself?

Your role model does not need to represent any person you now know. Research the characteristics of the imaginary hero that you will be. Once you've established this imaginary self-image, you'll be startled to see how others respond.

Need some confidence builders and some tests? Molloy, in his book *Dress for Success,* shows how the way we dress affects others.[1] However, because clothes symbolize certain kinds of behavior, unless we practice that behavior, we soon find the clothes no longer matter. It's the behavior implied by the clothes that eventually comes to the surface and really determines how others will react to us.

TRY THIS

1. If you're a man, put on a good suit and walk, with dignity and with the attitude that wealth is part of your life, into a Cadillac or fine car showroom. Maintain the role during the sales presentation. (Contrast the attention you get in this situation with the much less attention you would get if you entered another showroom and played a role that lacked dignity, poise, and elegance.)

2. If you're a woman, observe the respect you get when you display a dignified smile and a haughty presence in an expensive jewelry store. (Compare the attention you get with the attention you are unlikely to get when you enter a store looking wide-eyed and over-whelmed by the diamonds.)

3. During the next day on the job, display two or three characteristics that may not be typical of you. Observe what people say or do because these characteristics are unfamiliar to them. Watch how they react, showing the impact your behavior makes.

A FINAL WORD

Role modeling is a tool that requires some effort to master. It's easier to go back to the old ways. As you practice new behavior, you'll feel odd and uncomfortable. This is to be expected.

Presenting an image to the world may require changes in your normal routine. The surprised and uncomfortable glances of others as you become "different" to them may be disconcerting to you at first. But if there's a temptation to regress, resist it. You can become almost anyone you seek to be if you carry out your new role with care and allow yourself to be absorbed into it. Only those who are without direction, without knowledge of the role they wish to play, will remain snarled in the jungle.

TRY THIS

1. List on a piece of paper the characteristics that you wish to adopt in your life role and keep the list with you at all times.

2. Periodically review the list to see on which characteristics more work needs to be concentrated.

3. Score yourself periodically on how well you believe the role is being accepted by others.

4. Allow someone close to you to score you on how well you demonstrate a characteristic or behavior.

5. Revise the list periodically as you advance and succeed so that you continually grow within yourself and within the job.

When you play a new role, no matter how difficult it is, you eventually will be absorbed into it. As you start to find success, the role will become increasingly a part of you—to the point where you are totally immersed and comfortable with it. You'll need no further script. Your research will be completed, and the part will be yours.

And so will greater success.

NOTE

1. John Molloy, *Dress for Success* (New York: Warner Books, 1980).

Chapter 8

The Management Jungle: How Can You Maintain Discipline?

YOU PUNISH THE WRONGDOER NOT TO TAKE VENGEANCE
IRRATIONALLY, BUT TO CORRECT RATIONALLY.

Protagoras

8

Some years ago, the pollster Daniel Yankelovich found that an overwhelming 84 percent of all Americans feel a certain resentment that those who work harder and live by the rules end up on the short end of the stick.[1] It is obvious that managers today are dealing with employees who are far more cynical than their predecessors, and thus less likely to be trustful of management's intentions. There is in fact a complex new breed of employees in our health care institutions— employees who are far more assertive, far more knowledgeable about their rights, and far more certain about what they will do and what they won't do. These workers tolerate less, trust less, and want more. The big stick just won't work with them. In this management jungle, the pounding of chests produces yawns rather than fear.

THE OLD PUNISHMENT TOOL

Though you may feel that you are dealing with employees who, because they are represented by a union, appear to have a collective mentality, the modern worker is in fact more of an individualist than a follower. Today's employees will not learn by being bullied. If they stray from accepted institutional behavior— when they are chronically late, display absentee problems, disregard a rule or policy of the institution, refuse to follow an order, or are unproductive and uncooperative—the old management tool of punishment may be the least effective manner in which to exert discipline. In fact, it has become patently clear that *discipline* is no longer the name of the game; *correction* is! When a satellite varies from its intended course, the aim of ground control is to make changes, to communicate signals with the intent of bringing it back on course. Similarly, punishment per se is the least effective method of bringing employees around to accepted norms. Modern discipline must be corrective in nature.

74

As a manager, you are exposed to pressures from above to effect conformity, and to resistance from below to effect individuality. The name of the game is to ward off pressures from above to be oppressive and to develop a plan to change employees' attitudes, thereby also their behavior, while enhancing their need for individual expression. That's a large order. To accomplish it, you must understand your own biases; you must identify your present philosophy of interpersonal relationships; you must know where you're starting from.

TIME TO TAKE INVENTORY

What is my present view of discipline?

1. Do I believe that it is my role to get employees to toe the line?
2. Do I believe that most employees are trying to "beat the game?"
3. Do I believe that most employees are shirkers?
4. Do I see myself as a policeman?
5. Do I find it easier to turn my back on poor performance, than to meet the problem head on?
6. Do I believe that it is better to accept employees with poor attendance and lateness records than to face up to the reality that I may have to discipline them and/or terminate them?
7. Do I accept surface explanations for misbehavior?
8. Do I believe that discipline should be strict and severe?
9. Am I an "off-with-their-heads" supervisor?

If the bulk of your replies to these questions is positive, you are in the mainstream of leadership styles in our country. You are a ''Theory X'' manager, and you are probably on your way to an ulcer and a classic case of frustration and alienation. Douglas McGregor[2] discusses two theories about people and motivation. ''Theory X'' assumptions are the following:

1. The average person dislikes work and will avoid it as much as possible.
2. Most people have to be forced or threatened by punishment to make the effort necessary to accomplish organizational goals.
3. The average individual is basically passive and therefore prefers to be directed, rather than to assume any risk or responsibility. Above all else, security is important.

The second style, "Theory Y," has the following assumptions:

1. Work is as natural to mankind as play or rest and therefore is not avoided.
2. Self-motivation and inherent satisfaction in work will be forthcoming in situations where the individual is committed to organizational goals. Hence, coercion is not the only form of influence that can be used to motivate.
3. Commitment is a crucial factor in motivation, and it is a function of the rewards coming from it.
4. The average individual learns to accept and even seek responsibility, given the proper environment.
5. Contrary to popular stereotypes, the ability to be creative and innovative in the solution of organizational problems is widely, not narrowly, distributed in the population.
6. In modern business and organizations, human intellectual potentialities are just partially realized.

In practice, the big stick just won't work. Only children and immature adults believe that life is a contest of strength, a win-or-lose situation. The battleground of health care management is strewn with the cadavers of managers who constantly practiced adversarial techniques to obtain cooperation (the sham of angry "yes's" that await unguarded moments to express retaliatory "no's"). One does not mandate cooperation by punishing, by threatening, or by legislating.

A NEW PHILOSOPHY OF DISCIPLINE

There is no substitute for genuine agreement on the need to do it the right way. The challenge is to find the handle on employee cooperation. If you get into another man's skin, you are liable to see things the way he does, and you are liable to change your views.

How do you win cooperation and positive behavior from employees who break the rules. The first step is to reorganize, reevaluate, and establish a new philosophy of discipline.

TIME TO CHANGE WHAT'S ON THE SHELF

1. Recognize the cost of hiring, orienting, and training employees; it is worth your time and effort to get an

employee back on the productive and cooperative track.

2. Although at times discipline may have to be punitive, the most effective and meaningful approach is a *corrective* one.

3. When you discipline employees, remember "the whole world is looking at you." The other employees in your department will see when you give preferential treatment to one employee, when you come down hard on another. The rule of equality must be observed.

4. Certain differences in treatment may be defended; for example, long-term employees deserve a different standard of review. When you are dealing with such special cases, you must ensure that the employee's behavior is not merely a temporary and transitory apparition.

5. Make certain that the employee in question knew the rule, the right way to do the task, and had sufficient training and knowledge to behave properly.

6. Know your employees. If they believe you care, they are more likely to "do it the right way."

7. Get to understand your own management style and what effect it has on employee behavior. Too often, to quote Pogo, "We have met the enemy and it is us." Be honest in answering the question, Am I the problem, or part of the problem?

8. Compassion, dignity, and civility are the elements of effective leadership. Given a role model with those characteristics, employees will be less likely to cause disciplinary problems.

Taking Inventory

In the previous chapter we talked about positive monkey training. Nowhere is that more applicable than in applying discipline—or, to be more positive, in applying preventive discipline. Modeling serves a leader well in establishing the style that, when imitated, will produce productive and cooperative employees.

TRY THIS SOUL-SEARCHING EXERCISE

1. How many times in the last 12 months have I been late?

2. How many times in the last 12 months have I been absent?
3. How many times in the past year have I taken long lunch hours? (If it's too difficult to go back one year, make the inventory over the last three months.)
4. How many times have I left early, before the end of the work day?
5. How many times have I demeaned or criticized my boss in front of my subordinates?
6. How many times have I missed a deadline on a personal project? (Take a look at the top of your desk; can you see over it to the door?)
7. How many times have I had one too many drinks at lunch?
8. How many times have I been inaccurate in accounting for petty cash?

If you want your subordinates to behave properly, to be cooperative, to be productive, to be in on time every day and give you a 100 percent effort—then you must pass the test as a role model. It may well be that *you* are the enemy. It is up to you to set the proper pace, and you can set that pace in spite of a difficult boss who offers you a poor role model. You can set the tone in your area—in spite of the tone in the organization in general. You can build an *island of cooperation*.

The Key to Positive Discipline

The key to maintaining a positive disciplinary atmosphere has been available to us from the earliest research studies of behavioral scientists. Here it is:

THE KEY

If you treat people as individuals who, like you, need to have their dignity preserved in even the most trying situations (when they are being disciplined); if you constantly impress them with your concern for their welfare by simply asking them "why" something has happened; if you attempt to dig beneath the surface when problems arise; if you let people know when they have done something good as well as when they have done something bad; if you let them speak up, even if it makes you feel uncomfortable— then you will enhance their self-esteem, and other people's view of you as a human being will be enhanced.

Our own experience has led us to the conclusion that many of the disciplinary problems that plague management spring from work alienation. There has been much research in the area of work alienation. Let's simplify by once again embarking upon a soul-searching inventory of problems in the health care field.

TRY THIS

Ask your personnel department or your electronic data processing department to give you a list of employees in your department. Ask the personnel records department to send you the files on all of the employees in your department. Your department may be a large one, and you may have to do this piecemeal. Also, the bigger your responsibility, the more reasons you may find for not trying this. Forget the excuses, and face the music!

Now, it's time to get down to x-raying your department. Get a pad of accounting paper (8 to 10 columns will do). List your employees' names down the left side of the sheet. At the top of the columns, going across the paper, list the following titles: "Work Itself," "Pay," "Promotion," "Recognition," "Job Tenure," "Working Conditions," and "Demographics."[3]

Next, using a grading system with scores from 1 to 10, evaluate (make an educated guess) each employee's attitude under each of the headings. For example, for Employee 1, do you think that the work itself is fulfilling and meaningful to that employee. A score of 10 is the best rating. Do the same thing for each employee's pay, promotional opportunities, recognition the employee has received, the employee's job tenure, working conditions, and finally demographics. Demographics includes the employee's age, educational level, race, marital status, and so on.

Remember: this is your evaluation of the level of work alienation—of the level of fulfilling and meaningful work that each of your employees is experiencing.

Now comes the hard part. Review the personnel folders; review your files. What is the record of disciplinary problems experienced by each of your employees? How does this relate to their level of work alienation in the areas we have outlined? The name of the game is *interest*. You've got to know your employees. They must believe you care, that you take time in dealing with them as individuals.

Recently we came across a manager who complained about an employee who had been working for him for over 15 years. The employee had been absent more times in the past 6 months than in the previous 14 years. The manager also noticed that the employee was coming back late from lunch hours; in several "counseling" sessions, the manager reported to us that the employee reeked of liquor. Finally, the manager was forced to give the employee a written warning. Now the manager was faced with the unpleasant fact that there had been no change in the employee's negative behavior since the last warning. He told us, "I just can't stand this. If I let him get away with it, the other employees will know that I'll do the same with them."

We asked the manager how well he knew his subordinate. (Keep in mind that the employee had worked for this manager for 15 years.) The manager stuttered, hesitated, and finally said that he had too many employees in his department to get into their personal lives. (This reminded us of another incident, this time at a hospital where a doctor complained of workers' attitudes and how the people in his department were lazy and uncontrollable. When we suggested that she review the workers by using the grid outlined above, she said, "Don't bother me; I'm saving lives.")

We suggested to the manager that he take some time out and that, rather than hold a counseling session, he meet informally with the problem employee and find out why, after 14½ years of an unblemished work record, the employee was now experiencing difficulties. We were hesitant to ask the manager to develop a grid, such as the one above. We expected, however, that, from this single investment in one employee, the manager would get the message. And he did! His compassionate and direct concern uncovered a major change in the employee's home life. The pouring out of the problem by the employee—the catharsis—was the first step in solving the problem. The manager took the time to get advice to pass on to the employee and directed him to a service—a family religious counseling service. The employee was elated at the manager's interest.

Thus, discipline alone is not the answer. More often than not, the answer lies in determining the cause of the problem and assisting the employee by positive direction to remedy the problem. Years ago, in a study of what employees need most, high on the list was "help from my supervisor on personal problems." The reason it was high on the list is that supervisors have traditionally been remiss in providing such help. An unfulfilled need acts as a motivator—in this case, as a negative motivator.

When was the last time you told one of your subordinates that you were interested in that person as a human being? When was the last time you let your employees know that you're interested in their personal problems, that you see them as human beings, just as you are—frail and in need of appreciation and attention?

> In essence, what we are talking about is showing respect for people's humanness by communicating that respect in subtle yet powerful ways.
>
> *Richard S. Ruch and Ronald Goodman*

GUIDELINES TO EFFECTIVE DISCIPLINING

Disciplinary problems may spring from rules and policies that run counter to the prevailing customs in the workplace. If you do have disciplinary problems in your department, you should know why. Here are some of the reasons people in organizations act in unacceptable ways:

- Your subordinates may view the institutional rules and regulations as meaningless. To perform effectively, however, they must understand completely why certain rules are necessary.
- Your actions in dealing with disciplinary problems will carry over to future infractions. Rule violations will continue to occur if your subordinates believe that you are inconsistent as far as remedial action is concerned. You must prove by your actions that the rule is important, and that infractions will be dealt with.
- It is necessary that management make clear exactly what the institutions' disciplinary policy is, why it exists, and what the consequences are when it is violated.
- Not every violation is intentional. Be judicious in determining the cause of the violation. Otherwise, your heavy-handedness will result in a counterproductive response.

Here are some guidelines to effective disciplining:

- Your primary concern in disciplining employees is to salvage them, not to scrap them.
- Punishment is part of disciplinary action, but it is not the primary part.
- Correcting improper employee actions should be the main thrust of your disciplinary approach.
- Consistency is not the hobgoblin of a small mind. It is an essential ingredient in effective disciplining. Don't play favorites; the rule of equality of treatment should pervade all of your disciplinary actions.

- Remember the great line from Gilbert and Sullivan: "The punishment must fit the crime."
- The optimum disciplinary process springs from "self-discipline." It develops when employees trust their manager, when they feel that their job is important and appreciated, and when they feel that they belong.

Positive discipline encompasses the following sound managerial practices:

- Inform all employees of the rules and the penalties. The "why" of the rules is just as important as the "what."
- You are the role model. Do not play the game of "do as I say, not as I do."
- Do not be hasty in meting out discipline. Your role is primarily that of a fact finder. Remember, there are always at least two sides to every story.
- Judge the act within its context. Look for the least obvious motives and reasons.
- Discipline is a private affair. It is counterproductive to mete out discipline in public.
- There are two hallmarks of positive corrective disciplinary action: objectivity and fairness.
- We can add to that a third hallmark: consistency.
- Keep your eyes on the goal of the process: to correct improper behavior and salvage the employee.
- Punishment is a last resort—not the first.

Most observers of corporate life have come to realize that respect and care are primary ingredients of successful institutions. In the management jungle in which many of us find ourselves today, we would do well to eschew the negative aspect of disciplining, and instead pay more attention to cause and effect. Get to know the people who work for you; get to know them better than you know them now; get them to believe that you care about them as human beings; set the right role model for them. If you do this, the problem of disciplining will pale—not disappear, but rather lessen and take its appropriate secondary role.

NOTES

1. Daniel Yankelovich, Address to the National Conference on Human Resources, Dallas, Texas, 25 October 1978.

2. Douglas McGregor, *The Human Side of Enterprise* (New York: McGraw-Hill Book Company, 1960).

3. Special note is made at this point of the contribution to the authors' thinking by Richard S. Ruch and Ronald Goodman, "Work Alienation and Love on the Job," in *Image at the Top* (New York: Free Press Macmillan, 1983), 373.

Chapter 9

Sharing Control with Your Employees: Two Heads Are Better Than One; Three Are Even Better

ORDINARY PEOPLE ARE DYING TO MAKE A COMMITMENT.

John Naisbitt

9

Industrial democracy. This movement towards greater participation of employees in decisions that affect their every day lives—not the politically oriented thrust of some movements towards "Industrial Democracy"—seems to reflect the desire of free men to have greater control over their own lives. To the extent that this occurs, and to the extent that free men commit themselves to the goals of the organization because of their participation in its decisions, we are likely to have organizations of spirited vivacious people working together to accomplish their common goals—not bossed, not "hired," but free, committed men.

James L. Hayes

There is increasing evidence that, when employees are allowed to make some decisions about their work, they are more productive. It is a singularly important challenge to you, as a manager, to develop plans that increase worker participation. Such plans must develop a spirit of cooperation and teamwork as their end product. Your subordinates should be permitted—indeed, encouraged—to express themselves, and the critical nature of shared decision making must be sold down the line to the organization. Such sharing of decision making will positively affect productivity. When subordinates have a voice in significant problem solving activities—and therefore more responsibility for their own and their fellow workers' futures—they often experience a greater sense of interdependence among themselves, a larger awareness of the whole organization, a better time perspective, and a greater capacity to change the organization's internal makeup.

The loss of control over what employees do produces negative reactions from those same employees. This is often called alienation. It is clear that such alienation is greater in situations where subordinates do not—are not permitted to—participate in the decision making process. A concomitant reaction is a loss of initiative.

THE BENEFITS OF WORKER PARTICIPATION

WHAT PARTICIPATION CAN MEAN

1. The greater the number of competent judges, the greater the validity of their combined judgments.
2. Where participation occurs, there is a tendency for the participants to sharpen and refine an idea before it is accepted by the group; the group, in turn, is able to reject incorrect ideas that escape the notice of an individual working alone.
3. Tasks that are performed through cooperation, as opposed to competition, are more efficiently accomplished, with the persons involved exhibiting a higher degree of motivation and morale.
4. Group discussion using a democratic approach is more likely to alter opinions; conversely, attitudes are less likely to change when using an authoritarian approach.
5. Participation increases the likelihood that a goal will be set that is congruent with group-perceived values.
6. As a result of discussions involved in the establishment of a goal, the group members are more likely to have adequate knowledge of the nature of the goal, its worth to themselves, and its true attainability.

Most health care managers seem to avoid discussions of programs that increase worker participation. Many managers half heartedly participate in such discussions, and the employees quickly understand that their manager is not really committed to the program. Why do managers resist employee involvement? In most cases, it is because they themselves have not been involved in the planning of the program. More importantly, however, the reason can usually be traced to the loss-of-control syndrome. Managers often feel that if they have no knowledge of what an employee team will do and no influence over the team's activities, the result will be a threat to their own authority and position. Others believe that employees are not ''mature'' enough, not ''smart'' enough, not motivated enough to be involved in decision making.

You have got to be convinced that, in supporting a participatory management program, your job will in fact be made easier. You must recognize that the increase in effectiveness of the workforce for which you are responsible will redound to your credit.

An effective health care manager will attempt to organize and bring together the abundance of human competence to be found in the work arena. Less effective managers are often preoccupied with jargon, organizational charts, and routine policy making. They tend to defend the organization against "incompetent" employees. They continue to believe that employees really do not want to work, that all the worker wants is a fat paycheck. That may well be; but, if it is, it is a result of worker alienation, derived from a management style encrusted in an autocratic leadership model. In fact, if you believe that the average employee does not want to work and lacks ambition, your belief may well become a self-fulfilling prophecy. The desire for achievement, for the ability to make a difference at one's work, is a far more attractive concept for managers to deal with.

> If a worker is a free citizen in a free society outside the work place, involved in making decisions within his family and his community, why then should he be deprived of all those rights when he works in the work place?
>
> *Irving Bluestone*

THE JAPANESE SPINOFF

The ironic thing about worker participation is that the ideas now shaping Japanese approaches to industrial relations were imported from the United States. It was our behavioral scientists—from the Hawthorne experiments to Maslow's findings—who saw the enormous benefits of worker participation in decision making. Roethlisberger, who was involved in the early Hawthorne experiments, said that the big lesson of Hawthorne—the real Hawthorne effect—was the realization of the "big difference that the little difference of listening to and paying attention to the employees made to them."[1]

Douglas McGregor notes that the essential task of management is to arrange organizational conditions and methods of operation so that people can achieve their own goals best by directing their efforts toward organizational objectives.[2] Frederick Herzberg points out that, "if you want to motivate the worker don't put in another water fountain; provide a bigger share of *the job itself.*"[3] Chris Argyris warns us that, unless you increase the degree of discussion, confrontation, problem solving, and trust at the top, no movement is possible lower down.[4] Finally, Rensis Likert has taught us that the manager is the key factor in motivation.[5] The manager must make the workers feel that they are members of the team and that each one is personally important.

WHAT WE CAN LEARN FROM THE JAPANESE

1. Japanese senior management treats people as members of the corporate family, not as hired hands. In Japan the company is the people—not the shareholders—and accordingly employees are more important.
2. The Japanese emphasize management through shared values rather than through procedures and systems. This builds a mutual trust and confidence, and enables old friends and comrades to work well together with few details and procedures, and a powerful sense of direction.
3. The Japanese managers listen to the voice within their organization. This process is vital to the promotion of thinking that goes across normal organizational boundaries and reflects middle-management attitudes.

James S. Balloun

We have a lot to learn from the Japanese. The Japanese adapted a system that was originally developed, but then abandoned and never really implemented, in the United States. Today, the Japanese are making better cars at less cost, primarily because they have developed cooperative relationships with and between employees.

THE QUALITY CIRCLE MOVEMENT

Participation is accomplished by encouraging subordinates to offer suggestions about work flow and working conditions. It is enhanced by delegating responsibility. You maximize participation by creating an atmosphere in which subordinates can offer ideas, react to your ideas without fear of retribution, and participate in group decisions. A work group tends to elicit an employee's loyalty to the extent that it satisfies the employee's needs and helps the employee achieve goals. A worker tends to feel committed to a decision or goal to the degree the worker has participated in making the decision or determining the goal. The employee must understand why the decision has been made or why the goal has been set.

One of the methods used by the Japanese to improve productivity is the use of quality circles. This 30-year-old concept reaches into the depths of the organization to develop approaches and concomitant commitments.

QUALITY CIRCLE OBJECTIVES

1. to reduce errors and enhance quality
2. to create problem solving capabilities among broad-based groups
3. to promote job involvement
4. to optimize employee motivation
5. to change the supervisor-employee relationship from an adversarial one to a cooperative and harmonious one
6. to develop problem-prevention techniques
7. to promote personal and leadership development
8. to promote cost reduction

Quality circles use participatory management to the fullest. They are based on the premise that an organization's workers are closest to the problems—indeed, may be part of the problem—and therefore are best equipped to increase output and improve the caliber of work or service. They permit a broad base of employees the opportunity to speak up, in an atmosphere in which management is listening. A quality circle meets and, with the assistance of a facilitator and a leader, attempts to focus the group's attention on the analysis of specific problems and the development of recommendations to be given directly to the manager.

Each quality circle follows a three-step procedure:

1. *Problem identification:* Problems are identified; the selection of problems is a prerogative of the circle.
2. *Problem analysis:* This is done by the circle with assistance from selected experts.
3. *Problem solutions and recommendations to management:* Recommendations are made directly to the manager, using a communication technique called "the management presentation."

Many behavioral scientists who have studied worker motivation have concluded that positive results develop mainly from allowing employees to participate in the managing of their own work.

TRY THIS

1. Trust your employees. Expect that they will work to implement organizational goals given the chance.
2. Build employee loyalty to the institution. It will pay off.
3. Invest in training. Treat employees as resources which, if cultivated, will yield economic returns to the institution. This means developing employee skills. Implicit in this perspective is aiming for long-term employee commitment to the organization.
4. Recognize employee accomplishments. Symbolic rewards mean more than you think.
5. Decentralize decision-making.
6. Regard work as a cooperative effort with workers and managers doing the work together. This implies consensual decision-making.

Robert E. Cole

THE RISE OF PARTICIPATIVE MANAGEMENT

However, you do not need a formal quality circle to improve your workers' efficiency. You can do this on your own. You will be surprised when you ask your workers for suggestions; many workers will introduce facts that you might have overlooked.

It is the individual employee who is important. Therefore, you must treat all employees as individuals. If you do this, each employee's self-esteem will be increased, and, consequently, the employee will be more open, and less afraid of the consequences of such openness.

It's time for you to shift from being "manager as order giver" to "manager as facilitator."

Look around you and you will see that participative management is catching on. Of U.S. companies with more than 100 employees, 14 percent are now involved in such programs. Of companies with more than 500 workers, 44 percent have groups in which workers and supervisors discuss operations together. The results of these endeavors are astounding and deserve your examination: increases in productivity, decreases in absenteeism, positive feelings. Look at the successful organizations and you will see that they understand that employees respond positively when there is less, not more, control by management, when employees are not placed in narrowly defined jobs, and when they are not treated like unwelcome necessities but rather are given broader responsibilities, encouraged to contribute, and helped to take satisfaction in their work.

Close supervision has been proved time and time again to be counterproductive. That does not mean that you should just sit in your office all day and not care about what is going on in your department; it means rather that workers should have a degree of independence. They want to be treated as adults, which requires a fine-tuning of your knowledge of each of the personalities in your department. To some, you will have to be available on call; to others, your absence will cause anxiety; but, in most cases, your absence will encourage a sense of responsibility in your employees.

Balancing the concerns of your workers by not being overbearing is the key to enhancing their productivity. The optimum way to do this is to share your responsibilities with your workers. You must spend more of your time thinking about the creation and implementation of flexible responses to current problems. Such problems as staffing, productivity, and benefits restructuring must be addressed on a flexible basis. The key is constant attention to individual needs and contributions and to the building of morale within the organization.

In order to maximize your employees' motivation and opportunity to contribute, you must understand the pitfalls of the modern hospital organization. In most such institutions, there is a strong immediate pressure upon the individual to conform. There is a hierarchical structure in which the role model, the doctor, often is so preoccupied with personal expertise that all other concerns—like interpersonal relationships—are, at best, secondary. The resulting frustration and lack of need fulfillment lead directly to defensive behavior.

Thus, you must bring your employees into the mainstream of planning and implementing management goals. Dissatisfied employees will not produce the excellence we so desperately need.

More delegation is needed to build up employees' feelings about being part of the organization. The more we can do this, the better chance we have for commitment. The better the commitment, the more productive the effort. There must also be some relationship between performance and rewards. You may not be able to control the financial rewards—though keep in mind that you are an important factor in that area—but employees will nevertheless react positively to your concern for their well-being and growth in the organization. Though advancement is very important to today's employees, recognition shares that priority ranking in their needs.

Recent studies point out that negative responses and the lack of trust of employees can be turned around by:

- increased delegation
- more interactive communication
- more and better communication

TRY THIS

1. *Have positive outlooks:* If you believe workers are capable and want to do a good job it will be a positive self-fulfilling prophecy.
2. *Develop honest relationships:* If employees believe that you do not play a political game they will trust you.
3. *Develop a sense of partnership:* You must create opportunities for subordinates to feel that the institution's work is their work.
4. *Provide useful work:* This means providing opportunities for workers to grow.

J. Hall

It is clear that we have lost touch with our employees; we are not giving them enough information, especially about things that concern them most. A recent survey of working Americans by the Public Agenda found that less than one out of four jobholders says that he or she is currently working at full potential. Nearly half of all jobholders say that they do not put much effort into their jobs beyond what is required of them. Seventy-five percent say that they could be significantly more effective on their jobs than they are now. Nearly six out of ten Americans believe that people tend not to work as hard as they used to. From these findings, it is clear that most employees are underled and overmanaged.

A recent report by Hay underlines four important themes or feelings that people have:[6]

1. People feel significant; if they feel that their work is connected to the world, that there is meaning in what they are doing, they will be more productive.
2. Learning and competence matter; if people feel that they are allowed to make mistakes and that their superiors value learning, they will be more productive.
3. People are part of the community; if they feel that they are part of a "family," they will be more efficient.
4. Work is exciting; you must make your employees' work more stimulating and challenging—it is time to form a partnership with the employees under your supervision, to share your responsibilities.

Help thy brother's boat across and, lo! thine own has reached the shore.

Hindu proverb

NOTES

1. F.J. Roethlisberger, "The Hawthorne Experiment," in *Classics in Personnel Management*, ed. Thomas H. Patten, Jr. (Oak Park, Ill.: Moore Publishing Co., 1979), 23.

2. Douglas McGregor, *The Human Side of Enterprise* (New York: McGraw Hill, 1960), 47–48.

3. Frederick Herzberg, *Work and the Nature of Man* (New York: The World Publishing Co., 1966), 81.

4. Chris Argyris, "The CEO's Behavior" in *Harvard Business Review*, March/April 1973; *Leadership: Part 3*: 44.

5. Rensis F. Likert, "A Motivational Theory to a Modified Theory of Organization and Management," in *Modern Organization Theory*, ed. Mason Haire (New York: John Wiley & Sons, 1959).

6. Hay Management Consultants, *A Strategic Report Linking Employee Attitudes in Corporate Culture to Corporate Growth and Profitability* (Philadelphia: Author, 1984).

Chapter 10

Managers As Change Agents: The More Things Change, the More They Remain the Same

CHANGE IS INEVITABLE. IN A PROGRESSIVE COUNTRY, CHANGE IS CONSTANT.

Benjamin Disraeli

10

Change is the order of the day throughout the health care industry. No one knows that better than the supervisors and managers. In one way or another, we are all affected by organizational and structural changes, by changes in personnel policies and procedures, by changes in equipment, techniques, technologies, services, products, job content, reimbursement—the list goes on and on.

To resist change may be a natural human failing—but it is just that, a failing. To be successful as a health care manager, you must recognize the need for change; you must develop the ability to implement change by obtaining your employees' understanding, and you yourself must adapt to the change. Begrudging acceptance of change will be obvious to your subordinates. There is nothing more important in ensuring the successful implementation of change than a manager's excitement about the change's prospects and commitment to its implementation.

THE ART OF EFFECTING CHANGE

How do you increase the odds in favor of a smooth transition from one way of doing things to another? The first step is to understand why people do not get on board—indeed, why they resist change.

CHANGE: THE INGREDIENTS OF FAILURE

1. *Mystery:* Employees do not know the nature or effects of the change.
2. *Secrecy:* Little or no information is channeled down the line. After all, top management knows what is best. All that employees have to do is follow orders.

---

3. *Personalized change:* Employees perceive that the change is made only to affect them specifically, or that it is a punishment for something they have done.
4. *Pressurization:* The employees see the change as a speed-up, and they resist excessive work requirement based upon inconsistent or invalid standards.
5. *Poor planning:* The change is more a wish than a carefully constructed transition. (Try flying in a plane with one wing.)
6. *Lack of understanding of human nature:* Little or no attention is paid to the fears of employees when they must move away from old learned, ingrained habits and skills.

When you are asked to be the change agent, it is up to you to be the spokesperson for your employees. You must be the guardian of employee sensitivities to complex change. Understand that resistance is behavior intended to protect the individual or group from the effects of real or imagined change. Perceptions are important. When the organization dictates the need for change, facts alone will not alter the concerns of your employees. The adage, "the more things change, the more they remain the same," points up the atypical employee reaction: resistance born from lack of information and lack of participation in the development of change.

TRY THIS

The most important factor in initiating change and in overcoming resistance to change is to build a relationship of trust among managers, supervisors, and employees. In the paranoid world of the work arena, the key to developing trust is to be sensitive to employee needs. The need to know is primary. The need to be involved is equally important. You must start the process by asking yourself: What is my plan for ameliorating the effect of the change on the personnel involved. What is my plan for communicating that to them?

It is essential that the reasons for the change be communicated in detail. Do not mask those reasons; do not rationalize them. If the change's intent is to reduce costs, come out with it. If it is to increase productivity, there is nothing wrong in stating that out front.

> **TRY THIS**
>
> Essential to the selling of change is the encouragement of an exchange of concerns and information, including the setting up of situations in which employees will ask questions and such questions will be answered.

THE SUPERVISOR-EMPLOYEE CONNECTION

If you want to get employees on board, they must not be reluctant to ask questions about the change. It is their concerns you are addressing; it is their fears you must alleviate. A simple plan is to hold group meetings in which the reasons and details of the change can be explained. Smaller meetings, and even face-to-face discussions, should follow. There are two objectives for such meetings:

1. to explain in detail the why, how, and when of the change
2. to respond to the concerns brought forward

You, as manager, must be a part of the process. How can you be expected to sell change when you are not included in the relevant deliberations and developments? If you are not "in" on things, how can you expect to be an effective communicator for the institution in the process of selling and implementing the change? It is thus essential that you know what is going on, what is expected of you and your subordinates, and what the plans portend for the future.

> **TRY THIS**
>
> 1. Although most employees may resist change, if you understand the reasons for the resistance you can work with it.
> 2. To prevent or minimize resistance, you should explain in advance the need for the change, attempt to gain consensus, and establish a receptive frame of mind.
> 3. Never personalize the change. If you do, it will be a direct threat and a challenge to the employees. Indicate clearly and dramatically how the change will *benefit* the individual and the group.

4. Feedback is an important element in effecting positive change. It provides a way to determine whether you are "on target." Remember that what you mean to say is not always what you actually say or what the other person hears you say. In order to have effective feedback, your employees must believe that you will permit them to be frank and honest, without fear of criticism or loss of face.
5. Change is effected by communication, and half the process of communication is listening. The better listener you are, the better listening you will inspire.
6. Employees who participate in the shaping of a change are more likely to be receptive to the change and, therefore, more productive. The participation of employees is not a threat to your position. It can in fact be an effective management tool for you. *If your subordinates believe that you truly value their ideas, that you will consider their suggestions objectively, then they can be free to voice their concerns to you—then, and only then, will participation be effective.*

In any organization, it is the people involved who either make the implementation of change easy or difficult. The key to effecting a smooth transition is involvement. This starts with the level above you; indeed, a willingness to include supervisors in the planning stages is a cardinal precept for effective organizational change. If supervisors know what is expected, and why it is expected, they will be armed to present a clear picture of the change to their employees.

You are often the interpreter of communications that come down the organizational hierarchy. In this role, you are a key individual, the one who must give meaning to the stark words of policies and procedure manuals—particularly when they involve changes in day-to-day work methods. If you are bypassed in this communication process, the institution will suffer. You cannot market what you do not understand or about which you have not been consulted.

TRY THIS

1. Understand the reasons for the change in detail.
2. Believe in the change.
3. Begin by holding group meetings in which the reasons and details of the change can be explained.

> 4. Follow these group meetings with smaller ones in which you can explore with your employees specific problems and concerns and attempt to lessen the apprehension that will always be present in one form or another.
> 5. Follow this up with written communications to your employees.
> 6. Develop a feedback loop.

THE IMPORTANCE OF FEEDBACK

Feedback is an essential tool in the change process. It is a device for checking on whether or not you are "on target" with the goals of the change. It is often very difficult to convey meaning, especially when you are attempting to effect change. The full meaning of any message is affected by the total personality and experience of the employee receiving the message. Here, feedback is crucially important. You cannot fully appreciate whether the message has gotten across until the response is sent back. This feedback is a way of achieving understanding.

Feedback can be either corrective or confirming, either, "I was on target," or, "I was not on target." If you develop a continual flow of reliable feedback, you can decide whether or not your instructions to effect change have been understood and implemented. You then can make any changes that may be indicated.

> ### WHAT FEEDBACK IS AND WHAT IT IS NOT
>
> 1. Feedback is a mirror, not a directive.
> 2. Feedback is information that tells the receivers how their behavior either appears to others or affects the feelings of others.
> 3. Feedback is not evaluative. It is focused on specific behavior, not on the quality of the person; therefore, the individual's need to be defensive is reduced.
> 4. A little feedback is better than none at all, but the more feedback the better.

THE FEAR OF CHANGE

The real problem faced by health care managers in their attempts to effect change is the employees' perception that they might fail. Employees often are threatened by change because of fears they have about their inadequacies. Added knowledge and added skills can reinforce employees' feelings of well-being; they will then be less threatened by new assignments. The added knowledge and skills can be imparted by training employees in advance of the change. Sink-or-swim procedures have no place in effective management; if you wish to motivate employees to implement change effectively, you must give them a feeling that the activity is worthwhile—that the change is for the better. They must know the answer to the question: "What's in it for me?" Most important of all, they must believe that they can do the job as it has been reconstituted. To imbue confidence in your employees, you must hone their skills to a point at which they feel they can do anything. The resulting competent worker will be a gem! Most resistance to change stems from fear of failure; you can increase the odds of success by increasing the skills of your employees.

The list of horror stories about change continues to grow. Here is one that could be unfolding in any health care setting around the country, even as you are reading about it:

John was called in by his supervisor—the head of the ambulatory care department. He had not seen the supervisor for several weeks; indeed, he had had very little conversation with her over the past year. His supervisor greeted him with a smile and a handshake, saying, "John, sit down. It's good to see you. How is your family?" (John was not sure that she knew about the birth of his new son.) "It's too bad we don't get together more, but I do keep an eye on your work. How is that problem with your car?" (John realized that she was referring to an event that occurred some six months ago.) "Are you still active in the Community Chest drive?" (The supervisor did not even wait for a response.) "Well, it's certainly nice seeing you again, John. Oh, by the way, you are being transferred to our affiliated institution in _____ (a "close by" ambulatory care facility that was approximately 100 miles away).

John's reaction is predictable: anger, concern, frustration, and fear. All of these are normal reactions to change that comes as a surprise. John, like many other employees, was being caught up in a dramatic change and felt a loss of control.

Kanter tells us the most common reasons that managers encounter resistance to change:[1]

- *Loss of control:* When employees feel that they have no control over the events around them, they feel threatened.
- *Excess uncertainty:* When employees do not know the why, how, and when of change, they will resist it.
- *The "difference" effect:* People form habits and routines that are familiar. They see the need for extra effort in the projected change, and this causes resistance.
- *Loss of face:* People see the change as a personal comment on the way they were doing things. They believe the change is a result of their failure.
- *Concerns about future competence:* Here the worry is: "Can I do it?"

How can you overcome such fears?

TRY THIS

1. The key to effecting change is the commitment of those who will implement it.
2. If you want such commitment, you yourself must be committed.
3. Total, honest, and clear communication is the hallmark of successfully implemented change.
4. Implement the change in small doses. Reinforce the employees' sense of accomplishment at each stage.
5. Rewards should be plentiful. As the *One Minute Manager* tells us: "Catch somebody doing something right."[2]

CONCLUSION

Health care organizational expectations are not always in touch with reality. Change cannot be wished for, nor hastily overlaid on older organizational structures. Success is usually the result of a long, well-planned, and sensitive approach.

Every institution has its own unique culture. To ignore that culture when attempting to implement change is to invite disaster. Only a naive management would expect docile responses from employees when existing systems or policies are altered. To attempt to stifle or prevent honest differences in judgments about the process will be, at best, ineffective and, at worst, disastrous.

Managers should encourage conflicting views and not clamp down on dissenters. All dissension is not counterproductive. Also, you are not soft when you encourage openness. In short, the successful managerial change agent practices open and complete communication and encourages disagreement, so as ultimately to obtain agreement with commitment. When individual employees see the opportunity for increased involvement, career development, fair and appropriate rewards—then and only then will we succeed in achieving the institutional goal.

NOTES

1. Rosabeth Moss Kanter, *Managing Change—The Human Dimension*, a corporate educational video-tape (Cambridge Mass.: Goodmeasure, 1984).

2. Kenneth Blanchard and Spencer Johnson, M.D., *The One Minute Manager* (New York: William Morrow & Co., 1982), 39.

Chapter 11

Efficiency Is Not a Four-Letter Word: It's Cheaper by the Dozen

THE SUCCESSFUL CHANGE EFFORT CRIES FOR AN OPEN SYSTEM OF COMMUNICATION.

CHANGE WILL OCCUR MOST READILY AND EFFECTIVELY WHERE TEAM BUILDING IS ACCEPTED AS A MANAGEMENT PHILOSOPHY.

CHANGE EFFORTS WILL BE DESTINED TO FAIL UNLESS THERE IS EQUITABLE ACCEPTANCE OF THE RISKS INHERENT IN EXPERIMENTATION AND INNOVATION.

Gordon L. Lippitt, Petter Langseth, Jack Mussop

11

Readers who enjoy watching old films on TV probably will remember a classic that dates back to the late 1940s, entitled "Cheaper by the Dozen," starring Clifton Webb. The movie, based on the life of Frank Gilbreth, whom many consider the father of industrial engineering and management consulting, told the story of an executive who was obsessed with the need for efficiency. As the title implies, he believed that a family of 12 was the most economical and efficient, and throughout the film he continually goes through amusing exercises in scheduling his family to reduce the amount of time needed to do household chores.

As much fun as the movie is, the thought behind it is very real; the concept it develops is the foundation for modern industrial engineering methods. In fact, the word *therblig*, which is Gilbreth spelled backwards (with a slight variation), has become the term used by engineers to describe the time it takes a person to make certain physical movements, particularly of the hands and arms, as part of a work routine.

Gilbreth was a clever man. He was not only able to get many things done faster and better than most others, he also made a very good living to support his family of 12. Essentially, he applied common sense to the study of how things got done, and he came up with some tools that can be effective for any manager or, for that matter, for anyone who wants to cut the cost of doing things—an indispensable quality in a health care manager. In effect, his tools are procedural instruments for anyone who wants to get a greater amount of high quality work accomplished without increasing costs—another key characteristic of a successful health care manager.

SYSTEMATIC CHANGE AND IRRATIONAL RESISTANCE

Whether you call it industrial engineering, management engineering, or human engineering, the essential element is a systematic approach to improving how work is performed. It is one part common sense, one part business sense, and one part technical know-how. Paradoxically, in the real world of health care management, where efficiency is of benefit to everyone, the fact is that employees and managers alike resist the help that management engineers can provide.

The reason that most people do not listen to others who can help make them more efficient lies in the nature of human beings.

DON'T YOU LIKE ME ANYMORE?

To be told that the way we have been doing something is inefficient, unnecessary, too costly, or ineffective is an affront to our egos. It is an insult to our personal integrity, in that it implies that what we have been doing and how we have been doing it is not acceptable (or, at worst, meaningless!). We resist and resent being told that we are anything but the best.

What we need is the realization that our personal worth is increased as we become better able to do things and shorten the time it takes us to do them.

In the work setting, there is another reason why people resist efforts to make them more efficient. It is called insecurity. When employees believe that their work can be carried out faster, or perhaps eliminated altogether, job security becomes their prime concern. Why would people be interested in putting themselves out of work? Also, many managers are hesitant to take steps that might reduce the amount of power or influence they wield; reducing the number of employees working for them poses such a threat. Thus, efficiency is a complex subject. It is inextricably involved with human needs.

Of course, few employees—and even fewer managers—will ever admit openly that they are not supportive of "efficiency studies." Yet there is much game playing with different rationalizations, such as, "It's a good idea, but it won't work here," or "It won't save as much as you think," or "Quality of care will suffer." There are numerous variations on the same theme.

Resistance to a better ("different") way of doing things is frequently evidenced in behavior, as when, with the seeming support of those involved, a new system fails. The defense is, "We gave it a chance," and too frequently management is willing to accept the failure.

TEST YOURSELF

1. If someone volunteers to show how part of your job could be done in less time, thus leaving a "time vacuum," how would you react?
2. If told that something that you do either is unnecessary or unimportant, how would you react?
3. If told that a stranger, who is paid to find inefficiencies, will be working with you and study your job, how would you react? In all probability, poorly. Would you be

- defensive?
- insecure?
- resistant?
- cooperative?

THE INGREDIENTS OF SUCCESSFUL CHANGE

Now the bright side! Not every organization has a high level of resistance. An examination of the "winners," including some of America's leading money-making corporations and for-profit health care organizations, reveals organizations with strong employee support for improving efficiency and effectiveness. How did they "win" such employee support? Is it there for you to win?

IT'S ALL A QUESTION OF MOTIVATION!

When employees believe that there are personal advantages that outweigh the negatives, they are not only cooperative but, frequently, aggressive in seeking ways to change work methods. Find the key that opens the door to personal commitment.

As noted earlier, people are not afraid of change itself; they are afraid of the specific impact of the change upon them. Thus, if a change in procedure or work flow occurs, the impact on the individual employee may be very upsetting; it can lead to feelings of insecurity and doubt, and the disappearance of the psychological comfort of having settled into a normal work routine. No matter how brilliant an idea it is, or how beneficial it may appear to be, many people will still find the emotional trauma sufficient to resist it.

In the final analysis, the manager who continuously is able to improve work methodology while producing at least the same if not better quality in the end product is a manager whose career is on the rise. What is required is knowledge and use of the basic techniques of the industrial engineer, but in a form and manner that ensures personal commitment and employee support. Managers who have developed the trust of their subordinates will be more effective in introducing new methodology than the stranger on a horse (the industrial engineer). If you ask a person to enter a dark room, you must provide a searchlight!

THE CRITICAL TOOLS

To become a successful "efficiency expert," you must combine the need to make work more satisfying with the need to be more productive. Here, the critical tools are motivational analyses and motion studies.

Motivational Analysis

The first consideration in the quest to become more efficient is that time management and work efficiency are very much related. In both cases, unless you are very sure of how you will use the time saved as a result of the economies achieved, and unless what you choose is desirable to you, the odds are that you will not persevere and succeed. In short, unless the new way has emotional advantages, chances are that you will choose to do things the old way.

Moreover, unless your employees know how they will benefit—in terms of more enjoyable assignments, greater personal satisfaction, or less pressure—they will most likely resist the change. To understand such resistance, to address employee need fulfillment effectively, you will have to understand motivational theory. Given the need, a desired outcome, you will be moved to apply the relevant tools (even the hated industrial engineering approaches).

ASK YOURSELF

1. What things that are important to you are not given sufficient attention and effort?
2. What jobs or activities would be enjoyable and satisfying to do if there were enough time?
3. What business and professional reading and other developmental activities would improve your personal potential, if it was possible to do them?

4. What unhappiness or dissatisfaction about quality would you like to resolve?
5. What could be done with the money that would become available from savings achieved because of better ways of doing things?
6. What stress would be reduced or eliminated if present pressures could be removed?

These are on-the-job questions. But since increased efficiency and effectiveness can be accomplished in your personal life as well, why not apply the questions off the job as well?

ASK THESE QUESTIONS

1. What chores at home would I like to get rid of?
2. What unpleasant but necessary routines would I like to spend less time doing?
3. What "fun things" have I been unable to do because of other pressures?
4. What use could I make of money that I could achieve through efficiencies at home?

Once you have an idea of how you could fill in the vacuum so that desirable benefits come your way, the methodology of the engineer loses its mystique and threat and becomes instead a valuable tool. The first step is to define the target: You can't hit what you can't see! Also, remember that it's not foolish to wish upon a star. Today we travel through space, yesterday it was only a dream.

Motion Studies

We are creatures of habit; much of our behavior is by rote—unquestioned, repetitive, and, alas, all too comfortable. We go through life repeating the pattern, somewhat blindly, in many cases fighting to maintain a ritual for which we can give little logical defense. When trained on a job, we accept what we are taught and repeat the procedure compulsively, often not knowing or asking, "Why." We worry about departing from the sequence that has become the hallmark of "good" work (or acceptable work). After all, if our boss tells us, "This is the way it's done," and we're paid to maintain the pattern, why should we question whether there is a better way. To some managers, an employee who questions the normal modus operandi is not favored and may be viewed as a problem. How do we begin to break these old patterns?

Procedural Steps

TRY THIS

During the next few days, question yourself as to *where* you learned what you are doing and *why* you are doing it in *just that way.* Without evaluating whether there is a better way, ask yourself whether you have ever considered a different routine or whether the procedures you are following have become habitual, automatic responses that are rarely, if ever, questioned? This is a painful exercise, since it's easier not to ask such questions.

A motion study is merely a logical and methodical way of looking at what we do and why and how we do it. It provides basic information with which we can make changes in procedures to save time and effort and reduce cost and waste. It is carried out best by using a process called work flow analysis. This is a tool that is in the public domain. Industrial engineers do not ''own'' it; it is there for your use as well.

DO THIS
(It's Worth the Time and Effort!)

1. Think of a procedure or function that you would like to examine for the purpose of making it more efficient. (For a first try, choose something relatively simple to analyze, such as the opening of mail or a start-up routine at the beginning of the day, or, if you prefer, focus on an "I-wish-I-could avoid" routine, for example, the clearing of the dinner table or the washing of dishes.)
2. List each step (or "unit" of work) of the activity on the left side of an 8½-by-11-inch pad.
3. Be certain to go into detail (the "big" payoff comes from "little" changes). For example, opening mail may involve such steps as:

   • walks to in-basket across room
   • reaches left arm out to grab pile of mail
   • lifts mail out of basket

- covers with right hand
- straightens mail with both hands against body
- walks back to desk across room

Be specific and leave nothing out.

4. Study and analyze the steps or units of work that have been identified. (The closer you look, the more you'll see; the more you see the less likely you'll "accept" it.)

- What movements are unnecessary for carrying out the primary purpose of the procedure?
- What changes in sequence would reduce motion or time or would make better and more logical sense?
- What changes in movements would make the task easier and quicker to perform?
- Is there duplication of effort that can be eliminated?
- What parts of the procedure can be eliminated completely?

5. Relist the sequence with all the changes included.
6. Test the sequence over a period of time, to the point where you have learned and feel comfortable with the new or changed steps.
7. Evaluate the new procedure against the previous methodology. Which is easier, better, faster?
8. Adopt the new sequence, teaching it to others as appropriate.
9. After a period of time, evaluate the adopted procedure for improvement or the need for further refinement.

Potential Benefits

Obviously, the more complex the function or task being analyzed, the more complex and challenging the analysis will be. However, the more complex and important the procedure you are analyzing, the greater the potential for improvement in how the task is done. Thus, while you may want to make your first try on a relatively simple task in order to learn how to apply the approach, recognize that its real potential lies in its application to time-consuming and multifaceted functions. Keep in mind the benefits from this endeavor, but beware of change for change's sake. If the work pattern can be improved, made more interesting, made easier, and will reduce tension, your workers will jump on the "bandwagon of change."

MAKE IT A TEAM EFFORT AND
BENEFITS WILL MULTIPLY

As long as employees have an incentive (just as you should have) in making use of, or in some way benefiting from, the captured time and effort, they will be eager to participate in a motion study of their own work. Using an outlined form, or an 8½-by-11-inch piece of paper, give them opportunities to do similar studies on portions of their jobs that they believe could be improved by applying the motion study process.

Remember, a change in which you have had a role will more likely succeed than one that is mandated.

In today's paranoid world of health care management and DRGs, you may be hard-pressed to bypass philosophical explanations to employees about how improving efficiency will be best both for them and for the organization. Yet, the more you tell them "why," the better the commitment rate! The complexity of regulations and changed reimbursement systems continues to grow; in such an environment, employees will of course do what is necessary to preserve their own jobs, without necessarily viewing such action as being altruistic toward their organization. Yet, if a manager can work with a departmental staff to look closely at how *each* staff member can benefit, or can design a system of incentives, monetary or nonmonetary, the chances of a meaningful payoff will be greatly increased.

Benefits to employees and benefits to management are not necessarily mutually exclusive. You can wed the two, and, in the process, make the world your oyster! In some departments where staffing has been below levels that employees believe are adequate, a work flow analysis can benefit both the management and the employees. When employees—particularly those involved in direct patient care—understand how a motion study can help them carry out their professional assignments, they will be less likely to resent the process. Rather, they will be more likely to begin to think in terms of saving steps and reducing unnecessary effort. This is the what's-in-it-for-me syndrome. If the payoff is large enough, it may be worth the investment. And, the process is self-perpetuating and accelerative in its application; there are additional benefits in the form of less mental stress and increased allocation of funds for salary and benefit increases and the purchase of needed equipment and supplies. The challenge to managers is to make this clear to subordinates. Clarity regarding benefits begets commitment.

The Importance of a Meaningful Payoff

The real payoff from a motion study comes, not from procedural application, but from a belief in its necessity. It is only when the results of the study are seen as beneficial—by the manager and by the employee—that the process pays off. Knowing how to study a job—to break down its components, to revise, to improve, to facilitate—is not enough. What is important is to combine a knowledge of the tools of studying jobs with the tools of gaining acceptance. There must be understanding, there must be acceptance, there must be support, there must be participation. Finally, as a result, enthusiasm will flow and the big payoff will be at hand.

Forester warns us that whenever you plan to change things:

- Chances are you will make them worse.
- Chances are you will make them very much worse.
- And every so often you will cause a catastrophe.[1]

It is appropriate that these cynical comments be included in any discussion of time motion or work simplification studies. To repeat our earlier caveat: Beware of change for change's sake!

Keep in mind that most employees perceive time standards as oppressive. Only when the employees are involved in setting such standards do they make them work. If you establish credible standards, you are more likely to develop credible performance evaluations. Job descriptions based on performance standards have far more meaning than the usual routine job descriptions.

Standards developed through a cooperative effort of employees and managers are more likely to be effective. Similarly, efficiency efforts tied to incentives are more likely to succeed. With credible standards, it is possible to evaluate the quantity of work performed objectively and, in specific cases, to distribute incentive rewards for surpassing the standards, ensuring that the employees understand that the incentives are related to the productivity of each individual. In this area, some organizations have used innovative approaches, for example, the provision of release time for employees who complete their work assignments. The bonus of early release time provides the incentive to maintain productivity standards.

As one comes to understand the uses and benefits of motion studies, the more it becomes apparent that it is an ally, the more it becomes obvious that it should be used as an internal managerial tool—not one brought in by that "stranger on a horse.'' No one enjoys the presence of an outsider standing over one's shoulders, particularly a stranger who seems to be looking for speed as a payoff to management with no concomitant benefits to the employees. Employees see such studies as precursors of layoffs. Employees must have confidence, not only in the validity of the study, but also in its necessity and personal payoffs.

HOW TO MAKE THE QUEST FOR EFFICIENCY MORE EXCITING AND MORE ACCEPTABLE

1. The starting point is gaining employee acceptance. Arrange a training program. Cover the "how" as well as the "why."
2. Work with your employees so that they develop themselves to a point of full understanding of the benefits and value of studying their work habits.
3. Through group discussions, assemble suggestions for "better ways" of doing the work.
4. Suggest various approaches to studying jobs. Give the employees the tools to study their jobs on their own.
5. Give the employees the chance to make improvements in methodology. Encourage "silly" ideas.
6. Design rewards—both monetary and nonmonetary (be sure to get top management's commitment to providing these rewards!).
7. Remember that, not only are things cheaper by the dozen, they are also cheaper—and better—when done correctly.

The Feedback Process

To paraphrase Peter Drucker, the effective manager assumes that traditional measurement is not the right measurement.[2] Often, traditional measurements reflect yesterday's thinking. Drucker tells us that the best way to find the appropriate measurement is to search for feedback. This is not a mathematical exercise; it is a risk-taking one, one that springs from diverse and often conflicting views. If you study the way workers do their jobs, you must involve the workers. You must hear from them what and why they are doing things. You cannot start with the assumption that there is only one proposed course of action, one way to change things. And you must continually ask yourself, ''Is this change really necessary.''

You should make changes only if, on balance, the benefits greatly outweigh the costs and risks. Finally, you should make the change only after thoroughly studying how things are currently being done.

THE QUESTIONING MANAGER

The questioning manager is usually a mobile one. This manager walks through the department, is obviously interested, both in the work flow and in the worker. Such a manager is a "questioner." When looking at a particular work flow process, the manager is always asking:[3]

- Why is this being done?
- Is it necessary?
- What is being done?
- What is its purpose?
- Where is it being done?
- Could it be done elsewhere?
- When is it being done?
- Could it be done earlier or later?
- Who should be doing it?
- What skills are required to do it?
- How can it be done better?

Self-administered motion studies—if they are explained, implemented, and followed through with patience, understanding, and a great deal of assistance—can achieve for a manager a level of efficiency within the work group that may never have been anticipated. By making such an activity a team effort, the manager will strengthen the group as a working network of employees, and also enhance the manager's image as an effective leader. Employees who see how greater efficiency leads to job security and better job opportunities and makes additional money available for benefits and wages will soon recognize that the "efficiency expert" is not a villain after all. Efficiency experts will then become their best friends—particularly when the efficiency experts are themselves.

As the message in the Exhibit 11–1 ad reminds us, the essential credo, for both managers and employees, is to "aim so high you'll never be bored!"

Exhibit 11–1 A Managerial Credo for Change

Aim So High You'll Never Be Bored

The
greatest waste
of our
natural resources
is the
number of
people
who never
achieve their
potential.
Get out
of that
slow lane.
Shift
into that
fast lane.
If you think
you can't,
you won't.
If you think
you can,
there's a
good chance
you will.
Even making
the effort
will make
you feel
like a new
person.
Reputations
are made
by searching
for things that
can't be done
and doing them.
Aim low:
boring.
Aim high:
soaring.

Source: Reprinted with permission of United Technologies Corporation, Hartford, Connecticut, © 1981.

NOTES

1. Speech given by E.M. Forester, Massachusetts Institute of Technology, Cambridge.

2. Peter F. Drucker, "Effective Decisions," in *The Effective Executive* (New York: Harper & Row, 1967).

3. Gordon McBeath, *Productivity through People* (New York: John Wiley & Sons, 1974), 81–82.

Chapter 12

Catching the Will o' the Wisp: Making Time a Partner for Success

DOST THOU LOVE LIFE? THEN DO NOT SQUANDER TIME, FOR THAT'S THE STUFF LIFE IS MADE OF.

Benjamin Franklin

12

Many people moan about time being uncontrollable; they say that they can talk about time, but there is not much they can do to grab and hold its reins. It is like the elusive will o' the wisp. False! There are many things that can and should be done about managing time, and we all know people who have done exactly that.

> You are probably just as smart—if not smarter—than many of the rich and famous. The difference is that "somehow" they have the time to use what humble talents they may have. You have the same talents. And finding the time may be the least of your problems.

THE ELEMENTS OF SUCCESS

When you study the winners in life—those who get things done, who seem to be involved with everything—a not wholly unexpected combination of common elements emerges:

- motivation
- ability to evaluate efficiency
- ability to control interruptions
- skill in avoiding "meeting drain"
- skill in eliminating time-wasting habits
- ability to plan ahead

Motivation

The barrelful of excuses we often present when we are not able to do something is usually just a mask for the truth. What we did not find time to do we probably did not want to do! What better excuse is there than "lack of time" to ease our consciences and provide a socially acceptable way of avoiding the unpleasant. If there is something you have been intending to do but have put off because of lack of time, the suspicion is, that below the surface, you really chose not to find the time. On the job, we often tend to pace ourselves so that we accomplish during the workday those things that we either want or have to do, but not much more. The fact is that, if the day were moderately lengthened or shortened, you probably would accomplish the same volume of work. Even if your job involves managing employees involved in direct patient care, it is surprising to see how the pace of work can change so that more or fewer patients can be scheduled, or more or fewer services can be provided.

TEST YOURSELF

1. Do you tend to be more efficient and get more things accomplished the day before you head off for vacation?
2. More frequently than not, do you tend to "find" time to do those things that you enjoy the most?
3. Do you tend to find yourself fatigued or "out of sorts" when faced with parts of your job or with chores that you do not enjoy?

You should not be embarrassed if you answered all three questions with a resounding yes. You are normal. But your answers underscore the importance of motivation in "finding time."

DO THIS

1. Identify those chores, assignments, or actions that you earnestly and emotionally *want* to do but have not done.
2. List the tasks in the order of desirability, the first item being the most desirable, the last item the least desirable.

> 3. Decide for yourself how strongly you feel about doing
>   the tasks.
> 4. If you are emotionally stimulated by this exercise, you
>   are ready for the next step.

If, however, the exercise did not enable you to come up with a stimulating list, do not be surprised. The reason is the same reason that most people have trouble finding time—they are just not "turned on." If there is nothing that grabs you emotionally, accept the situation until another occasion arises. Accept it, because at the moment the motivation factor just is not strong enough for you to "find" that elusive time.

On the other hand, once you have a goal of doing something that excites you— something that you really want to do—it is time to fill in the vacuum. The odds now are that you will find the energy and the determination to succeed in doing what is necessary to find the time.

Ability To Evaluate Efficiency

How Time-Efficient Are You?

> With full respect to Ben Franklin, a minute saved is a
> minute closer to success.

The cliche, "hard work is not always good work," is a reminder that how we use our time may be the only difference between ourselves and others. In spite of what we may feel, we really have more time than we think we have.

There are times when, faced with a deadline, we wish there were some extra hours in the day, or at least some extra minutes in each hour. Maybe there are! It all depends on how your "personal time clock" has been constructed. If there is too much "time filler," you cannot get as many minutes into the hour. A time filler is also known as:

- a time leak
- a fool's errand
- force of habit
- official policy
- the way we always do it
- a ritual

A reduction in the amount of time filler has the same effect as adding minutes and hours to your day. You remove frustration, while "finding" time you never knew was available.

Consider the situation of the store owner who is about to paint lines in a new parking lot. With careful planning before beginning the job, it becomes possible to accommodate a greater number of cars. By clever planning to reduce the amount of unused space (the filler), more cars can be accommodated without enlarging the parking lot. Retailers will tell you that a good parking space planner is worth big dollars in increased customer traffic. In fact, many hospitals faced with a problem of insufficient space for employee' parking have redrawn the lines in their employee parking lots and have thereby "found" extra room. Similarly, by planning to utilize the presently unused space (the time filler) on your personal time clock, you free up minutes and hours to accomplish tasks for which there formerly would have been no opportunity to undertake.

An expeditious way to start your search for hidden time is with a well-used tool: the time audit. However, some modification is called for, since the typical time audit is tedious, boring, and frequently discarded within a few days—if not within a few hours. The traditional method requires you to keep track of everything you do, usually in intervals of 10 to 15 minutes, for a period of from one to two weeks. In the hectic environment of most health care institutions, this method must be replaced by a more practical approach—one that gives you almost instant feedback as to whether or not you have too much time filler, or whether you are caught in a "time sieve" that is robbing you of the minutes and hours that can be put to much better use.

The Time Audit Updated

Try *time interval measurement* (TIM—the missing *e* in the acronym is a reminder of the space that can be dropped from your clock). Here's what it is: Conceptually, you change the way you get paid. Instead of a salary for a basic work week (even if you are a workaholic, your work supposedly can be done within a stipulated time frame), you are paid for each thing you do in terms of *its relative value*. That is, the pay you receive is determined by the value of the work actually performed, rather than by the amount of work done or the amount of time spent or the job.

If you succeed in doing work with a value at least equal to the amount of your salary, you get your full pay. If, however, you spend your time doing things that do measure up to the value of the job, you get paid only up to the amount that your efforts were worth. Doing low value work for the full week would leave you unhappy—and a bit poorer. On the other hand, filling the week with accomplishments that are worth more than your current pay could bring you a larger pay check than normal. Thus:

Time interval measurement is a method by which you can determine your true value on the job. It enables you to discover where the extra filler can be found that has prevented you from earning the larger pay check, from doing those "extras" that previously you were unable to accomplish.

To use TIM off the job, divide the interval of time you want to evaluate by a target amount equivalent to a personal value. Whenever you find that you are over or below the target amount, you will have a fair idea of how well you are measuring up.

Most men and women who have earned reputations as high achievers have learned to shift the value of their time from low to high. This is a logical move. Put two managers side by side—with the same job, same level of responsibility, same level of pay. The two set out at the beginning of the year: Manager A spends most of the work day completing assignments with high values. In fact, this manager either has delegated low value functions to others or has found ways to do them expeditiously with a minimal amount of time. Manager B spends most of the day bogged down with low value functions, because "there is no one else to do them," and is unable to give full attention to responsibilities with the greatest values. Both managers work hard, and what they do they do well. The only difference is that Manager A has succeeded in working at the parts of the job that are most valuable, and Manager B has not. There is no contest when the time comes for promotion, salary increases, or professional rewards. Manager B's defense is that "if he didn't do it, it wouldn't be done." This is a valid rationalization, and Manager B deserves sympathy. But the fact is: the value of Manager B's time does not measure up to that of Manager A.

DO THIS

1. At the top of an 8½-by-11-inch piece of paper, place your salary divided by the so-called "normal" work week of your oganization in minutes. The value of each minute you are on the job is thus:

$$\frac{\text{weekly \$}}{60 \times \text{hours in work week}} = \text{value per minute}$$

2. At least two or three times each hour, stop what you are doing and write down what you were doing during

the previous few minutes. (You may wish to take measurements at greater frequency or measure larger time blocks; just be sure you get a good sampling of your daily routine without making spot audits too frequently.)

3. Measure the job value of those minutes. Are they worth more or less than the value of the minutes actually invested? (This is determined by subtracting the payroll value of the time worked from its estimated job value per minute.)

4. Record the plus or minus value on a separate sheet.

5. To get a more accurate measurement, have a secretary, a colleague, or another employee determine when the measurements will be made. At those times, have the other person ring a bell, call you, or give you a signal. This ensures the compilation of a more random, and probably more realistic, set of measurements.

6. Continue this exercise for a minimum of two days and a maximum of two weeks in order to see patterns form and to get sufficient insight into the value of your time.

7. At the end of the period, total the values you have recorded.

8. Determine your payroll value by totaling the values recorded on your score sheet and dividing it by the number of minutes audited, then multiplying the result by the number of minutes in the work week. The final value ÷ number of minutes of audit × total number of minutes in the normal pay period = the amount, more or less, you were worth in relation to your pay check.

9. If your final score is a minus number, you have plenty of filler to work with. If you have a plus number, feel good—momentarily—and move on to the next section of this chapter.

If you are like the majority of managers, both within and out of the health care industry, your TIM will reveal that too much of your time is spent on the type of assignments and functions that diminish your effectiveness and worth. This should worry you, it should concern you—it even should scare you—since it is a black cloud over your future and your ability to do things with the greatest payout to you. If you are in the minus category, the sooner you can shift the balance from low value to high value, the sooner you will increase your worth to yourself and to your organization and free up time for doing those things on your motivational list.

You have common sense. Use it! If you do not see a clear path to dealing with those low-yield, time-consuming activities, consider the following ideas as starters:

- Delegate (see Chapter 6).
- Don't do the low-value functions.
- Change someone else's job to include some of those functions.
- Seek ways to do those functions more expeditiously; use the advice of others as appropriate.
- Phase the functions slowly out of your routine.

Note: if the things you *want* to do have sufficient motivational value, the checklist provided in the subsequent section on planning will serve as a good starting point.

Ability To Control Interruptions

Many times we enjoy an interruption that gives us a break from routine. Too frequently, however, interruptions are uncontrolled and throw us off stride. Moreover, interruptions are disturbing, not only because of their unpredictability, but because of the time they "rob" from our day. Yet interruptions are inevitable; they cannot, nor need they, be eliminated. Indeed, in a health care environment, interruptions and emergencies are a part of normal life. What is needed is a way to control them so that others do not get into position to own your time.

DO THIS

1. On an 8½-by-11-inch sheet of paper, keep a record of every interruption that occurs during each work day. Include phone interruptions—they can be the most harmful. Indicate the amount of time that, unexpectedly, you had to give up.
2. Score each interruption. If the time you spend during the interruption was worth the value of the minutes involved, give it a plus. If the time was not worth the value of the minutes spent, give it a minus.
3. Analyze the seriousness of the interruptions. More minuses than pluses indicate that action needs to be taken.

It is too simple to say that barriers must be built against interruptions. Instead, more definitive planning is needed. There are a number of devices that can help you in this planning.

TRY THIS

1. If you note that most interruptions are by the same persons (including bosses), have a direct conversation with them concerning the impact of the interruptions—and some possible remedies. An individual who interrupts for good reason but who stretches out the time might be asked to stick to business and eliminate extra minutes taken up by small talk. (This can be done with tact and understanding.) In some cases, individuals may be asked to restrict their visits to certain times of the day so that you can better plan and give them uninterrupted time, rather than be squeezed for time.
2. Handle phone interruptions in a similar manner. Callers can be requested tactfully to stick to the business at hand, or they can be asked, either by you or by a secretary, to call at certain hours of the day.
3. Use help. Not everyone is fortunate enough to have someone else intercept the interrupters; however, if you have this advantage, use it. Secretaries can provide a formidable barrier by steering unexpected visitors and callers to others who might also have the answers or information being requested. Secretaries can relay messages so that interruption time is minimized. They can also help prevent unnecessary telephone call-backs by either supplying information or making the calls for you. You do not need, nor do you want, an "iron curtain;" a "soft veil" can be just as effective.

If you really mean business, your careful control of interruptions will remove much of the filler from your hourly clock.

Skill in Avoiding "Meeting Drain"

"Meeting drain" describes the feeling a person has after participating in a meeting that takes more time from the day than it gives in fair return. It is the drained feeling one has when the meeting has gone on interminably long, or when you feel your attendance was neither necessary nor desirable. Some otherwise very time-efficient people can lose their advantage by allowing meeting drain to offset whatever gains they have made because of their efficiency.

Of course, if it is a command performance, *go*. However, too often, you will find yourself in a meeting you had hoped would be profitable, but you are disappointed. In such cases, you can still fight the effect of "meeting drain" by increasing in certain ways the value of the time being spent at the session. Here are some tips to reduce the effect of meeting drain:

- *Be a good member of the group.* Change your lack of interest into interest, and gain valued time, by participating fully with ingenuity and your full mental resources. Others will respect you for your participation, and you will probably be surprised by how much value you get from a session that you were ready to write off.

- *If you are bored, take notes.* If you have to be there, listen with "money ears." Jot down ideas and thoughts you hear. Boredom has a way of closing down the listening senses; yet there may be a gem or two that you might have missed. Writing forces you to listen more intensely.

- *Make certain you are fully aware of the agenda.* Calling the chairperson in advance to learn the agenda will help you prepare (or make the decision not to attend). Indeed, such advance research may entice you to attend and benefit from a meeting you were ready to avoid.

- *Help move the meeting along.* Even if you are not chairing the meeting, you can make a positive contribution by helping others stay on the subject and move to solutions. Encourage discussion and suggest solutions without taking over or risking embarrassment to yourself or someone else.

- *If it will help in the future, talk to the chairperson after the meeting.* Many people are sensitive to criticism, but when you offer to help them improve their ability to run a meeting (rather than tell them what went wrong), they usually are appreciative. Conference leadership is a skill; if people do not possess the skill but want it, they will welcome your suggestions and they will thank you when, as a result, they feel more confident about themselves in future meetings.

- *When you conduct your own meeting, ensure success.* Be sure everyone knows the agenda in advance; be sure the participants want to be there; be sure everyone comes prepared. By inviting only those who will benefit in some way from the discussion, your meetings will develop a reputation of being worthwhile.

- *Assess the meeting.* Determine what you should do better next time. Determine what action you can take or suggest to help someone else.

Meetings are a valuable tool in the management process. But as with any other tool, how they are used is a measure of their value.

Skill in Eliminating Time-Wasting Habits

We frequently are victims of our own habits, and we thereby lose sight of many of the details in daily routine. In addition, there are habits and actions we perform that, though they once had sound justification, no longer are valid or worthwhile. This is particularly characteristic of the health care field, where professional protocols are basic to action.

By conducting a different type of audit of our time, it is possible to identify time-wasteful habits and to eliminate functions and routines that consume large amounts of time. It is possible to find holes in the time sieve that drain away our time. It is possible to patch the leaks in the sieve! When you plug the time leaks, you free up many minutes and hours for use on higher priority or more enjoyable tasks.

Here is a checklist of time-wasting habits that may make a difference between doing and wishing; the more you have, the more you are wasting your most precious commodity—time:

- avoiding or putting off unpleasant or undesirable duties
- doing unproductive things because they are comfortable, easy, or long-term habits
- starting a job when you know (or suspect) you will be unable to complete it or will be interrupted
- doing things too thoroughly, including developing more details, facts, and other minutia than is necessary or worthwhile
- allocating too much attention, effort, and time on work with low priority or value
- beginning a job or assignment without necessary or sufficient preparation or planning
- allowing meetings, conferences, and conversations to wander, drag on, or go off on tangents
- allowing personal phone calls, conversations, or socializing to take place or continue beyond the courteous stage
- making improper use of the phone by allowing lengthy conversations or repetitive conversations to take place
- doing personal work on the job that can be (and should be) done on your own time
- volunteering for or accepting more responsibilities and duties that can possibly be scheduled or achieved

- doing things that could be delegated to others
- doing things that could be done in a better or more expeditious way
- keeping records that are unnecessary, too detailed, or duplicative of other available data
- performing your daily routine without anticipating or building in flexibility to handle crises, emergencies, or the "unexpected"
- spending too much time on low priority or unimportant work with subordinates
- spending insufficient time with employees to ensure their work is being done properly and on time
- spending too little time with subordinates to discuss their problems and the impact of those problems on their jobs
- spending too little time coaching and counseling employees in building a strong team
- allowing others to interrupt you, interfere with your work schedule, or woo you away from your work
- stretching out assignments because of fatigue, boredom, or lack of interest in what you are doing
- allowing coffee breaks, lunch periods, and other off-the-job time to extend into or interfere with the work day
- doing things in such a way that they have to be done over

Here are four rules to help you use the above checklist:

1. Keep it with you for reference at all times.
2. Whenever you do something that appears on the checklist, make a note of it on your "time-sieve" record sheet (a plain 8½ × 11 inch sheet of paper will do nicely).
3. Once weekly, review the list to determine how much time you may have lost and what the impact was on your routine.
4. Take steps to plug the holes in your time sieve, keeping in mind that, for each function you eliminate (each hole you plug), you are making additional time available, either to increase your value or to start moving on achieving those goals that heretofore were unattainable.

Ability To Plan Ahead

When you have "found" sufficient extra time to do the things you need and want to get done, you are, in some ways, like the builder with a yard full of building supplies. Putting it all together requires a plan. Such a plan will enable the strength of your motivation to show itself. If you have been able to plug the leaks in your time sieve, and if your use of TIM has given you insights upon which you can capitalize, a sound plan will now provide the map you need to steer you along the path to success.

The simplest and most commonly used map is a carefully prepared "to-do" list that identifies your targets for the day, for the week, and perhaps for the month. To-do lists come in many sizes and shapes. However, the form itself is not important; it is what is on the form that will enable you to prosper.

> Too frequently, a to-do list is a "wish" list; but, though wishes have a place in our lives, they are usually symbols of a naive dreamer.

A sound to-do list should indicate those things that you have identified as necessary accomplishments for a particular day. It should indicate the tasks to be fulfilled, the amount of time that will be needed to fulfill them, and the time of the day targeted for their achievement.

A well-prepared to-do list becomes a score card. When you ultimately find that you are batting close to 100 percent each day, you will know you have succeeded in controlling your time.

AND NOW, SUCCESS

Take stock. If you have succeeded in eliminating much of the time filler that was plaguing your routine, if you have succeeded in plugging the time sieve, if you have reduced the negative impact of interruptions while shifting most of your efforts from low- to high-value work—you are not only worth more to yourself and your organization, you will also have those additional minutes and hours to pursue those things for which you previously did not have time. It is literally the time to go into action and reap your rewards!

> Lying on the beach is delightful—at the proper time. "Lying on the beach" while at work diminishes you as an individual and as a manager. Those managers who lie on the beach while you are making things happen will be left in your wake.
>
> The word *efficient* describes those who get things done when they are supposed to get them done. The word can apply to *you*! When you have sufficient control over your life clock, you will feel that you have indeed captured and harnessed the will o' the wisp.

Chapter 13

The Moon, the Stars, the Pot of Gold: A Short Primer for Setting and Attaining Goals

THE MAN WHO UNDERSTANDS WHAT HE MUST DO, AND WHO IS ENCOURAGED TO DO IT, ACCOMPLISHES FAR MORE THAN IS EXPECTED BY HIS BOSS OR BY HIMSELF.

Raymond F. Valentine

13

"They" said it was folly for Fulton to think he could build a steamboat; "they" said it was impossible for a man to succeed in reaching the moon. "They" are all around us—doubters, cynics, the faint of heart. If the "they" had their way, we might still be back in the dark ages; if "it can't be done," why would anyone spend time and effort inventing, exploring, and discovering! But that's not what's happened. Instead, marvels and new creations emerged; mankind progressed. Fulton built his steamboat; Neil Armstrong set foot on the moon; and medical miracles are made nearly every day. How?

Many wonderful things have come from dreams. Yet attaining goals is more than dreaming. What separates the dreamers from the doers is planning—practical, logical, and well-proven planning. You can use a sound plan of action to achieve goals you may have thought unattainable, and you will find it a very formidable tool when faced with goals that are difficult and complex in nature.

When confronted with a task about which we know little, it is tempting to reach out for help from those who have had experience or success with a similar endeavor. However, when Fulton began building his steamboat and NASA started planning for a trip to the moon, there was no one around with the relevant experience; there was no one available to give advice because the needed technology had not yet even been invented.

> You do not have to be an expert, nor do you have to know in advance the answers, to achieve what "they" say can't be done.

Expertise and know-how are not always the prime requirements to achieve a goal; in many cases, the strategy you utilize enables you eventually to achieve the expertise and know-how required to accomplish the task. Here, the focus on strategy becomes critical. Here's how to do it.

THE FIVE STRATEGIC STEPS TO SUCCESS

Step 1: State Your Goal in the Form of an Accomplished Result

Confidence that you will achieve your goal is easier to attain when the goal is pictured as an accomplished fact. When so viewed, it becomes possible to visualize having succeeded and to "taste" the feeling of victory. For example, the traditional method of stating a goal might be "to get a college degree at night" or "to lose weight." If the goal is stated as an accomplished fact, it becomes a "BA degree in business management from a university." Similarly, "to lose weight" can be viewed in a more motivational way as "loss of 18 pounds."

DO THIS

At the top of an 8½-by-11-inch paper (you might prefer an 8-by-5-inch card), write the goal you want to achieve in the form of a completed accomplishment. State it as it will be after its achievement. (One can visualize John F. Kennedy looking at the following words on a piece of paper somewhere on his desk during the time he was still campaigning: "John F. Kennedy, President of the United States." Some have hinted he did just that; he could "taste" the pleasure of victory.)

Step 2: Decide How Strongly You Want To Achieve the Goal

The reason many health care executives have found that management by objectives frequently fails as an effective tool is that the process becomes a ritual, bereft of the motivational factor. People must have a reward as compensation for effort. Whether that reward is in the form of self-satisfaction or something material depends upon the individual's values. In any event, if there is one single thing that prevents people from achieving the goals they set for themselves, it is a low level of motivation—a less-than-consuming desire to fulfill a need. The potential value of the reward that they will receive does not equal the effort, inconvenience, or sacrifice involved.

DO THIS

Write down on a piece of paper "what's in it for me" when a certain goal is achieved. Write out the emotions you will feel and the tangible rewards you will receive; note every inducement, large or small, that will make the effort worthwhile. This is a private list; be frank with yourself. Some of the items will be meaningful only to you. If vanity is a motivator, accept it. What is important is whether the rewards in store "turn you on" sufficiently.

For example, if your goal is a master's degree, you might write:

- I'll have a feeling of enormous satisfaction and achievement.
- Others will respect me for doing something they did not.
- No longer will I have that negative feeling about myself—a feeling of inferiority because I do not have a graduate degree.
- There will be many jobs open to me that are more exciting and pay more than the job I have now.
- There will be a special diploma on the wall that my children and others will admire.
- All the doubters who thought I couldn't do it will have to admit that they were wrong.

Similarly, the motivators for a loss of weight might read:

- The way I'll look will make me proud of myself.
- I'll look younger and more attractive.
- I'll no longer feel shame because of my flab.
- My fatigue will be replaced by energy.
- I will be healthier because I am slimmer.

Remember: If the motivations don't "ring your bell," you had better acknowledge the probability that you will not persevere in achieving the goal. This involves the "balance-beam" approach to decision making. To illustrate: when

Ted Kennedy declined to run for the presidency it was because he just did not feel the goal was worth the enormous expense in time, effort, and money. In contrast, John F. Kennedy won the presidency, in spite of being told he could not do it, because his high level of motivation—his ego drive and desire for success—gave him limitless energy to carry out the tasks that lay ahead. This is the motivation cycle at work.

Step 3: Identify All Barriers That Stand between You and Success

In spite of being highly motivated, one may find that a goal eludes achievement simply because of the lack of a strategy to achieve it. There may be indecision about where or how to start. Here, there is a tested solution used by high achievers:

Essentially, to achieve a goal, identify and remove the barriers.

Quite simply, when you remove the barriers, there is nothing left to prevent you from attaining success. When JFK decided to seek the presidency, two of the most formidable barriers were the opposition of his state's Democratic Party leaders and the widely held belief that a Catholic could not win the presidency. Kennedy identified these barriers and removed them. In effect, instead of initially spending large sums of time, money, and effort appealing to voters, a move that would have been mistimed, he worked for two years to make certain that a majority of the state chairpeople—those who could wield the most influence at the Democratic Party convention—supported him. In the same way, he and his associates addressed the barrier of the "Catholic myth" and ultimately negated the religious question to the point where it no longer could hold him back.

Similarly, when NASA set out to get a man on the moon, it identified the barriers that had to be overcome and assigned teams to develop solutions. For example, a major concern was that there was no metal available that was sufficiently resistant to the heat generated when a space ship reentered the atmosphere. Ultimately, those involved with the problem came up with a heat shield, constructed of a ceramic material, that could do the job. The barrier was removed—and, incidentally, Corning Ware was born!

DO THIS

On your goal achievement planning sheet, list every conceivable obstacle, barrier, or block that might stand in

---

> your way. Whether the barrier is psychological, financial, or physical, whether it is formidable or minute, it must be listed; for it is only when these barriers are removed that you will achieve your goal.

For example, the barriers that might stand in the way of achieving a master's degree might be:

- lack of time needed to attend classes and study
- lack of money needed above normal spending
- lack of confidence in returning to school after being away
- uncertainty over what courses to take

The barriers that may face you in an effort to lose weight are probably mainly emotional, and yet, perhaps for that reason, even more formidable:

- a love for and desire to eat sweets, cakes, candy, and ice cream
- a life-long habit of nibbling and making late-evening raids on the refrigerator
- ease in gaining weight quickly—possibly a slow metabolism
- the notion that, "this is the way I am, the way everyone else sees me; if I lost weight, I'd look different"

Planning in removing barriers is made easier if there is specificity in identifying obstacles. Thus, instead of saying the barrier is "the need for money" or "time," the barrier should be stated as "the need for $1,000 a course, plus $55 for fees and books."

The question of time calls for further research—which of course is precisely the point of being specific. When the amount of time needed is stated in terms of the hours during which the courses are given and the time needed for travel and perhaps to compensate for leaving work early, it becomes possible to deal with the real world. If this is not done, many barriers are not seen in their specific dimensions and thus become merely nebulous clouds of uncertainty and intimidation.

> When barriers are stated as specific and clearly identifiable obstacles, they lose much of their mystery and become manageable—both physically and emotionally.

Step 4: Set Priorities for the Barriers in Terms of Importance and Difficulty

Part of the strategy in achieving goals is to be certain that energy is spent productively. When you put the work in order of priority, you minimize the possibility of wasting time, money, and effort. There is no sense in removing barriers that can be confronted more easily later, after more immediate concerns are fully addressed.

> There is no sense worrying over the color of a house before the house is built. First things first.

The setting of priorities in dealing with barriers permits you to evaluate the time necessary to remove them and then to prepare realistic target dates and schedules. It provides a full perspective of the tasks involved. It also permits a realistic evaluation of how well-prepared you are mentally, financially and professionally. In effect, the setting of priorities gives you a springboard for action. Done properly, it can enable you to be "off and running," with a high level of confidence.

DO THIS

1. Analyze each obstacle, indicating any further investigation needed to amass sufficient facts and obtain assistance.
2. Number the barriers in the sequence they should be addressed. In this way, your effort is directed toward building to a success by eliminating the most critical stumbling blocks first. There are times when several actions can be undertaken at the same time; these should be identified.
3. Set up a schedule to which you can adhere. The schedule should be firm. Remove the temptation to change the schedule; if you allow postponements, you may be condemning your effort to failure.

Step 5: Move into Action

You know your target. You can feel and sense your rewards. You have identified the barriers and obstacles in your path, and you have determined their order of importance. You have a timetable. These are the essential elements of success—the foundation for doing the impossible and conquering the unconquerable.

Now, the concentrated effort, the mobilization of resources, and the sound thinking come into play. Your efforts are concentrated, your energies are channeled in one direction, and you have peace of mind because you have a purpose and a plan.

A WORD ABOUT ACHIEVEMENT

The effort to remove a barrier is usually an individualized—indeed, a customized—one. This is particularly true if you are aiming to achieve something that has no precedent or are exploring unknown waters and have no experience or insight to help you find the best way to move forward. Such an effort can be a lonely undertaking. In such cases, when the problem to be resolved appears particularly formidable and challenging, a team effort is the best way to move forward. Each of us has a given supply of imagination; the stimulation of that supply by others in a team effort enables us to rise above the lower limits of imaginative effort. Thus, when you have completed the five steps described in the previous sections and are faced with making the next move, consider the following additional approaches to make the job easier, less lonely, and more satisfying:

- Ask the advice of others who have an interest in your success.
- Reduce the need for meetings by having others give you their ideas in writing.
- Set aside a specific amount of time on a regular basis to concentrate on actions to remove barriers.
- Explore different options and approaches with those for whom you have respect. And listen to them.
- Be prepared mentally for disappointments, surprises, and setbacks.
- Persevere.

IF YOU'RE EVER DOWN, DISCOURAGED,
OR UNSURE

Keep your list of motivators handy. Review them and reinvigorate yourself. Many lesser people have accomplished bigger tasks than yours.

DO IT

Chapter 14

Random Thoughts on Achieving Excellence

A MANAGER WHO KNOWS THAT HIS SUBORDINATES ARE HIS EQUALS BECOMES THE EQUAL OF HIS SUPERIORS. IF HE DOES NOT TEACH HIS SUBORDINATES TO FEAR HIM HE MAY NOT LEARN TO FEAR HIS SUPERIORS. IF HE RESPECTS THEIR LIVES, HE MAY LEARN TO RESPECT HIS OWN. IF HE PERMITS THEM TO DISSENT, HE MAY ARROGATE DISSENT HIMSELF.

Earl Shorris

14

The inability of many Americans to find purpose in their work can help to create the shift from the work ethic to a self-fulfillment ethic. Most people no longer want to work hard. They demand more leisure hours in which to seek some other purpose or pleasure under the catchall contemporary concept of self-development.

Gail Sheehy

We differ from Sheehy's statement—not in the finding, but in the cause of the phenomenon. It may well be that people today are looking for acknowledgment and seek out some form of self-development. The major difference from Sheehy's conclusion is on the motivation of people: Most people do want to work harder, but they haven't found meaning in their jobs. If, as Freud tells us, man's connection with reality is his work, then finding meaning in our lives means finding meaning in our work.

Caring about people is the be-all and end-all of organizational strength and success. Treating workers fairly and enunciating and practicing values that recognize the need, worth, and fears of employees are not sentimental doublespeak. Such behavior is not opposed nor detrimental to the productivity and financial viability of an institution; on the contrary, it is an essential part of scientific management. When planning becomes an end unto itself, rather than a means, when the financial statement is bowed down to by sitting executives, when the importance of acting as role models is overblown by chief executive officers, we are witnessing mere lip service attention to the voices of the employees.

Modern management advances the simple notion that workers who perform fragmented and routinized functions over which they exercise no control quickly exhibit the classical manifestations of alienation—they have higher absenteeism, they are less productive, they are more sullen, they are hostile. The sheer simplicity of this causation is overwhelming. The pundits of planning, of strategic and quantitative analysis—the scientific managers—nonetheless decry the general "lack of discipline and respect for authority," the "laziness," and other undesirable attributes that supposedly characterize the working population. In doing so, they focus on effects and avoid the effort to understand causes; they fail to consider alternate interpersonal relationships.

CARING: THE HALLMARK OF SUCCESSFUL LEADERSHIP

There is no question that what we are witnessing in our institutions and in the country in general, is what Eli Ginsburg has described as a deepening and broadening concern with aspects of people's lives, individually and collectively, that were previously given short shrift. Clearly, it is time to pay attention to the entire gamut of our employees' needs!

Caring counts! People are concerned that they will be regarded as insignificant. Workers want managers to appreciate their contributions. If workers become alienated, they do so because they have no stake in the outcome of their work; they feel that they have no control over the outcome they seek. Often, their managers care little about recognizing their workers' accomplishments and give them as little responsibility as possible. They are aware that they themselves, and in turn their own bosses, are treated the same way. Indeed, many of the bosses in the hierarchy might well be catalogued in Lombardo and McCall's "rogues' gallery":[1]

- *Snakes in the grass*—bosses who lack integrity and generally cannot be trusted
- *Attilas*—little Napoleons or martinets who sit on people
- *Heel grinders*—bosses who treat others like dirt
- *Egotists*—bosses who know everything, won't listen, and parade their pomposity proudly
- *Dodgers*—bosses who are unable to make decisions and shirk responsibilities
- *Incompetents*—bosses who just do not know what they are doing and won't admit it
- *Detail drones*—bosses who go strictly by the book and delight in detail
- *Rodneys*—bosses who just "don't get no respect"
- *Slobs*—bosses with personal habits, appearances, or prejudices that are intolerable to others

Yet, in spite of all of these rogues, many managers are able to exert a leadership style that is directly concerned with the willingness of their subordinates to contribute effectively to the overall goals of the organization. These successful managers display certain leadership traits.

LEADERSHIP TRAITS OF SUCCESSFUL MANAGERS

1. willingness to take risks
2. willingness to make decisions—even if unpopular
3. concern for the human aspects of management
4. concern to protect the dignity of others
5. broad flexibility about subordinates and the organization in general
6. a "high touch" style of management—sharing kudos, giving rewards
7. willingness to make mistakes, and to admit that they have made mistakes
8. high concentration on the development of subordinates
9. realistic perspective, laced with a sense of humor
10. innovative attitudes and behavior
11. confidence
12. ability to criticize constructively, to take criticism without becoming paranoid

PRESSURES TO CONFORM

In most institutions there is a strong immediate pressure upon the individual to conform. Such pressure is counterproductive. Unfortunately, it is often perpetuated by the pyramidal structure of hierarchy in the traditional health care facility. Such a structure is based on a formal, "military" organizational approach: omniscience and omnipotence lie at the top of the pyramid (often, unfortunately, there is also continual argument over whether the power lies with the medical staff or with the administration); and all planning, budgeting, and decision making flow from the top down.

It is time to develop a new and different approach! As noted earlier, the real lesson of Hawthorne—it is now 50 years since that famous study on efficiency was conducted—was the recognition of the big difference that the little difference of listening to and paying attention to employees made in job productivity. Hawthorne taught us (though we have been slow to absorb the implications) that workers are social creatures. We of course have to pay them competitive salaries, but just as important is their need to find security, independence, participation, and growth through their work. This means breaking out of the typical institutional structures, job definitions, and reward systems; it means finding a straighter road.

THE CALF PATH

One day through the primeval wood
A calf walked home as good calves should
But made a trail all bent askew,
A crooked path as all calves do. . . .

The trail was taken up next day
By a lone dog that passed that way;
And then a wise bellwether sheep
Pursued the trail o'er vale and steep,
And from that day, o'er hill and glade,
Through those old woods a path was made.

And many men wound in and out,
And dodged and turned and bent about,
And uttered words of righteous wrath
Because 'twas such a crooked path . . .

The forest path became a lane
That bent and turned and turned again;
This crooked lane became a road,
Where many a poor horse with his load
Toiled on beneath the burning sun,
And traveled some three miles in one . . .

The years passed on in swiftness fleet,
The road became a village street;
And thus, before men were aware,
A city's crowded thoroughfare. . . .

Each day a hundred thousand rout
Followed this zigzag calf about
And o'er his crooked journey went
The traffic of a continent.

A hundred thousand men were led
By one calf near three centuries dead.
They followed still his crooked way
And lost one hundred years a day;
For thus such reverence is lent
To well established precedent.

> . . . For men are prone to go it blind
> Along the calf-path of the mind,
> And work away from sun to sun
> To do what other men have done.
> They follow in the beaten track,
> And out and in, and forth and back,
> And still their devious course pursue,
> To keep the path that others do.
>
> They keep the path a sacred groove
> Along which all their lives they move;
> But how the wise old wood-gods laugh
> Who saw the first primeval calf.
>
> *Sam Walter Foss*

A STRATEGY FOR SUCCESSFUL CHANGE

There is a strong and continuing temptation to move along in familiar ways, to accept things as they are "because that's the way they are." However, you should be ready to move off the path that others have taken. You should be ready to think about new and different things that you can do. You should be ready to speak up. Franklin Roosevelt once said that new ideas cannot be administered successfully by men with old ideas.

The successful organization of the coming decade must address a changing environment and, therefore, must be willing to change itself. There is a crying need for such flexibility. Problems involved in staffing, productivity, and rewards must be addressed on a flexible basis. The key to success is constant attention to the recognition of individual needs and contributions. You must develop systems to maximize the opportunity for employees to display their innate motivation to contribute. The challenge is there.

PREMISES FOR THE DEVELOPMENT OF A
STRATEGY TO RESHAPE THE TYPICAL HEALTH
CARE ORGANIZATION

1. emphasis on organizational informality and fluid flexible lines of communication and reporting relationships
2. sharing of "managerial prerogatives" with line supervisors and workers on a systematic institutionalized basis

3. multifaceted human relations programs that quite literally pervade the organization
4. a managerial ethos that insists on the constant recognition of the importance of the organizations' employees
5. constant ongoing efforts to reassemble fragmented
   functions and to share with the workers the control
   over the manner and circumstances in which these
   functions are performed
6. antiauthoritarian employer-employee relation structures that encourage decentralized innovation and
   initiative at the line level

The Critical Targets

What can you do to improve the way people work? There are two critical points of attack to effect such a change: the people at the top, and the people in the middle.

The People at the Top

First, you must become a trust builder. Little or no trust can develop among tightly controlled workers. You cannot expect that such workers will trust you and give you the commitment you need to achieve excellence. The rigid application of management tools—such as restrictive and narrowly defined jobs, tome-sized strategic planning manuals, and inflexible and impersonal personnel policy manuals—will quickly make your employees feel that they are only a necessary evil, not a partner, in the delivery of patient care. Trust is built by CEOs who share the prerogatives of their job. It cannot be built by paranoid executives. The more support you give your subordinates, the more support they will give you. The pervasive abuse of authority and power, the view that employees are subservient and reluctant followers in need of control and discipline, is the antithesis of trust building.

A TRUST-BUILDING MANAGER:

1. looks for common ground
2. is not easily angered
3. feels positive
4. encourages boat rockers
5. is a "truth teller"

Increasingly, reports indicate that top management is becoming more and more isolated from the work force. There is a need for a more gregarious management style; managers must come out of their offices and into the larger institutional environment. To build up an atmosphere of trust, executives must find their own values within the context of the work arena.

People admire responsible and honest executives. Also, self-reliant, trusting, and decisive supervisors produce efficient subordinates. Parkinson describes what happens when such leadership is lacking—when there is failure at the top:

> We find everywhere a type of organization (administrative, commercial or academic) in which the higher officials are plodding and dull, those less senior are active only in intrigue against each other, and the junior men are frustrated or frivolous. Little is being attempted. Nothing is being achieved. . . . It is the disease of induced inferiority called Injelititis. . . . The first sign of danger is represented by the appearance of an individual who combines in himself a high concentration of incompetence and jealousy. Neither quality is significant in itself and most people have a certain proportion of each. But when these two qualities reach a constant concentration represented, at the present, by the formula I_3J_5—there is a chemical reaction. The two elements fuse, producing a new substance that we have termed "injelitance." The presence of this substance can be safely inferred from the actions of any individual who, having failed to make anything of his own department, tries consistently to interfere with other departments and gain control of central administration.[2]

Too often, we are confronted by such people in our organizations. We must get rid of these debilitating administrators. We must learn how to use an anti-injelititis serum—to quarantine such individuals from our day-to-day activities.

The Managers in the Middle

The second critical point of attack to effect a positive change in the organization is the managers in the middle. There is no position more frustrating than that of the middle manager, the manager who must perforce represent top management to the employees and the employees to top management. Such individuals find it very difficult to move from control to commitment in the work place; no one is in a more difficult position to take on such a challenge. Yet, no one is more potentially influential in the drive to increase productivity, lessen worker alienation, build morale, and reduce costs than the middle manager.

Too often, CEOs and top management fail to appreciate the middle manager's key position as a change agent. Indeed, the middle manager is often the forgotten element in the organization. The key to reversing this situation, to developing strong middle managers, is training. Most methods now used to train supervisors perpetrate authoritarian (counterproductive) managerial styles. Such traditional authoritarian methods just will not work. The development of self-reliant, trusting, and decisive supervisors will have as its end product an efficient work force. Thus, it is time for CEOs to understand the value of their middle managers' ideas, to consider their suggestions objectively, and to permit them to voice their concerns without fear of retribution.

With the advent of large institutions and accompanying complex employee relations problems, middle managers—though armed with techniques and methods far superior to those of their predecessors—have paid a high price for overspecialization. They are pressed to get things done at the sacrifice of achieving understanding. Today, managers must be developed to be collaborators. The legitimacy of the unshared hegemony of top management must be questioned.

Those who occupy the middle ground have a lonely job. Even with a diminished and weakened union movement, many unionized employees have more power than their supervisors: at least someone—the union—is there to speak for the employees! There is also a unity among blue collar workers that is not found among managers, especially those in the middle. Often, the lack of direct access to the top—indeed, the absence of even a mechanism for such access—as a means of sharing concerns and making middle managers a part of the decision-making, top management team compounds the problem. Finally, middle managers are frequently too far removed from their own subordinates. The result is often feelings of insecurity and wavering loyalties.

Given such conditions, it is not difficult to understand why many blue collar workers turn down promotions to supervisory jobs. The workers perceive the lack of flexibility and freedom at the entry and middle levels of management; and they prefer, perhaps understandably, the relative security of repetitive mindless work.

In his seminal book *Working*, Studs Terkel interviews Larry Ross, an ex-president of a conglomerate, who says:

> The corporation is a jungle. It's exciting. You're thrown in on your own and you constantly battle to survive. . . . The danger starts as soon as you become a—manager. You have men working for you and you have a boss above. You're caught in a squeeze. The squeeze progresses from station to station. I'll tell you what a squeeze is. You have the guys working for you that are shooting for your job. The guy you're working for is scared stiff you're gonna shove him out of his job. Everbody goes around and says, "The test of the true executive is that you have men working for you that can replace you, so you can move up." That's a lot of baloney. The manager is afraid of the bright young guy coming up.[3]

This is not an uncommon perspective. All the more the pity. Remember: your subordinates are not your enemies. Not only are they not your enemies, they in fact look to you to protect their interests. As Buskirk observes:

> Subordinates want protection from attack by others in the organization. They will accept deserved criticism from their immediate supervisor but expect in return to be free from harassment from other executives in the organization. And they expect their boss to go to bat for them when the occasion warrants. Woe to the manager who fails to support (fight for) his group when the need arises.[4]

Support your people and they will support you. Respect your people and they will respect you.

It has been said that to have self-respect is everything. Without it we are nothing but unwilling slaves at everybody's mercy, especially those we fear or hold in contempt.

The Search for Excellence

Some 400 years ago, Baltasar Gracian, a member of the Society of Jesus, wrote about the need for satisfaction from one's work:

> Most things depend upon the satisfaction they give others: an appreciation is to talent what the west wind is to the flowers, breath, and life itself. There are occupations which enjoy public acclaim; and there are others, even though more important, which receive no recognition: the former because done in the sight of everybody win favor: the latter, even though they possess more of the rare and the worthy, remain unnoticed because done in obscurity; they may be venerated but they receive no approbation.[5]

The importance of recognition cannot be overstated. The fear of obscurity, of insignificance, is pervasive in modern life. Because of such feelings of obscurity and insignificance, people's confidence can be destroyed. The challenge of leadership is to create and develop that confidence and provide meaningful work for subordinates. This can be accomplished when the leader has developed a positive self-regard. Bennis and Nanus note that positive self-regard is related to maturity. The resulting "emotional wisdom" is expressed in five key skills:[6]

1. the ability to accept people as they are, not as one would like them to be
2. the capacity to approach relationships and problems in terms of the present rather than the past
3. the ability to treat those who are close to you with the same courteous attention that you extend to strangers and casual acquaintances
4. the ability to trust others, even if the risk seems great
5. the ability to do without constant approval and recognition from others

If you wish to achieve excellence, you must learn to trust others; you must systematically get to *know* your people. One of the problems with performance evaluation is that it is a long look *back* rather than a long look *forward*. When you develop self-regard you become an effective leader. When you, as a leader, then deal in terms of human possibilities, you are on the road to excellence.

NOTES

1. Michael M. Lombardo and Morgan W. McCall, Jr., "The Intolerable Boss," *Psychology Today*, January 1984, 45–48.

2. Northcote Parkinson, *Parkinson the Law* (Boston: Houghton Mifflin, 1980), 175–176.

3. Studs Terkel, *Working* (New York: Pantheon Books, division of Random House, 1972), 405–406.

4. Richard H. Buskirk, *Modern Management and Machiavelli* (Boston: Cahner's Books, 1974).

5. Martin Fisher, trans., *Gracian's Manual* (Springfield, Ill.: Charles C Thomas, 1945), 70.

6. Warren Bennis and Burt Nanus, *Leaders* (New York: Harper & Row, 1985).

Chapter 15

Urban Renewal: Changing the Work Setting

THE WAYS IN WHICH THE WORK PLACE IS REVAMPED, THEREFORE, ARE NOT A MANDATE OR EVEN SIMPLY A BY-PRODUCT OF THE TECHNOLOGY BUT A RESULT OF CONSCIOUS CHOICES.

Harley Shaiken

PARTICIPATION IS NOT A PROGRAM OR A TECHNIQUE; IT IS AN ALMOST MYSTIFYING PHILOSOPHY OF CHANGE FOR HELPING PEOPLE TO FULFILL THEMSELVES.

Richard Dangen

15

Everybody talks about achieving excellence. The whole country is directing its attention to productivity. However, the key to both excellence and improved productivity lies in the often shaky hands of managers. The new breed of employees need something better—a new setting. It is time for urban renewal. On this issue, Kanter asks some critical questions:[1]

- How can the desires of increasing numbers of people (women, minorities, and the highly educated) for "meaningful work" that produces "career growth" be accommodated?
- How can openings be created for younger educated workers to exercise their skills, when older workers fail to step aside and have the legal right to retain their jobs?
- Over time, as the workforce ages but the trend toward increased education continues, how will desires for opportunity and power be accommodated for this large pool of competitors, all of whom feel eligible for the small number of existing high-level positions?
- Who will fill the entry jobs as the population ages and people feel "too educated" for "mere entry jobs"?
- What steps can be taken to ensure that people feel that they have sufficient power in their jobs, in terms of their treatment, dignity, and respect and a voice in decisions?

THE NEED FOR NEW STRUCTURES AND RELATIONSHIPS

Kanter suggests that perhaps the most promising solutions lie in worker-management, problem-solving structures, such as joint labor-management committees that deal with productivity as well as quality-of-work-life concerns. These structures would usually include:

- steering committees for overall coordination, composed of representatives from different levels, including management leaders and unions where applicable
- task forces and/or action groups to address specific issues
- an advisory group that provides opportunities to inform the rest of the system or to tap other usable resources.[2]

It is important that you, as a manager, be flexible in your thinking about employee relationships. The labor force is changing. By the end of this century, women will account for about two-thirds of the growth in the labor force. That labor force will have increased by some 25 million workers, and most of these workers will be in their prime ages—between 30 and 49. They will be much better educated than ever before. This certainly must direct our attention to a change in style—since better educated workers have higher expectations.

Surveys show that over one-half of all college graduates feel underutilized in their jobs, compared to only one-third of noncollege graduates. These more educated workers are looking for more challenging jobs, and they want to be listened to. Clearly, the successful manager in the closing decades of this century will need to be more sensitive than ever before.

REQUIREMENTS FOR A NEW SENSITIVITY TO EMPLOYEES

1. Managers must have positive outlooks, honest relationships, and a sense of partnership with their employees.
2. To be effective, supervision must be based on the belief that people are not by nature passive or resistant to organizational needs. The manager's responsibility is to enable employees to fulfill their own needs and goals, as well as the organization's needs and goals.
3. Managers must be open with their employees. Employees want to know what is going on, and they want to know what the manager thinks. Communication skills are critical in achieving excellence.
4. The manager must listen to the employees—even if it is disquieting, even if they are critical, even if they say something the manager doesn't want to hear.

> 5. To achieve independence, the manager must develop a sense of independence among the employees, insisting that they take on more responsibility. The sharing of responsibility in no way diminishes the manager's position.
> 6. Managers must involve their employees in goal-setting. Goal-setting is not a skill that is limited to board rooms and CEO suites.

To modernize, you need not tear down the old structure. The most successful urban renewals have been accomplished by a process of building on the old, by building around the old, by renovating the old. The first step is to take inventory. Here are some soul-searching questions for managers who want to change things:

- Do you understand your institution's goals? Do you have confidence that they can be attained?

- Do you understand that confusion is your enemy, that clear understanding and clear communication about goals and responsibilities are essential?

- Are you open with your immediate supervisors? (Remember the "emperor's new clothes" syndrome!)

- Are you willing to ask for clarification, for additional information, without feeling the request is a negative reflection upon you?

- Are you a team-spirit builder? Do you care about the team? Do you care about the individuals who are part of the team?

- Do you find refuge in operational emergencies? (Sometimes make-work is the last refuge of a scoundrel!)

- Do you make time for the people who need you? Or is there a moat around your office (your castle)? Do people say, "My manager is always available to me"?

- Are you always looking for ways to move your people ahead? Or do you keep good people down? Do you hide the gems so that no one else can have them?

- Are you familiar with the "cornucopia of fruit"? Do you have "bananas" available to hand out to those who accomplish something? (Remember that a human being lives for recognition and that you can be the bestower of such recognition.)

- Do you keep in mind that the most precious possession a worker has is personal integrity? (A person's reputation is a precious possession! Respect a person's integrity, and that person will respect yours.)

- Do you find time to deal with employees' personal difficulties? (No one comes to work out of a vacuum; everyone has another world separate from the work arena. If you are a good listener, the opportunity for employees to share their personal difficulties with you often provides a catharsis for them.)
- Are you developing an understudy for your job? Or are you so threatened that you continually concern yourself with the "competition"?
- Do you need to be involved in every decision? Or do you delegate responsibility to your subordinates? Do you use every opportunity to build up in your employees a sense of importance about their work? Do you place real responsibility on your subordinates?

THE NEED FOR A REALITY-BASED PERSPECTIVE

Before undertaking this urban renewal project, based on the above inventory, let's take another view—with a different lens—of you as a manager. From this new perspective, to become a successful manager, you must understand and apply certain basic assumptions and principles:

- At times you may not feel it, but you have more status than you think you have; employees see you as the "boss."
- Although you are "in the middle," you can develop a productive and efficient relationship with the people you supervise.
- To be a successful manager is to master the art of consultation. People who participate in planning, who feel free to make suggestions, and who are consulted in advance about change are more likely to be productive.
- Although your people see you as the "boss," you need not hover over them. Get to know your people and give to each the instruction, information, and evaluation that are needed. Not everybody needs you all of the time; but be available when you are needed.
- There are two pay systems operative in every institution: (1) the normal pay system built on competitive wages and fair differentials and (2) the other "pay" system that you personally are in charge of, that includes appreciation, communication, and opportunity for fulfillment.
- It should not be a threat to you if many of your employees want more challenging work. Don't "hoard" good workers. Make and search for opportunities for advancement and more challenging work for the people who produce for you.
- Although the work is important, in the final analysis people-centered supervisors move ahead in successful organizations. "Needs" appreciation is the first order of the day for people-centered supervisors.

- Managers achieve success by encouraging their subordinates to make suggestions and participate in decision making. Such encouragement is enhanced by maintaining a nonjudgmental attitude toward employees who offer suggestions and a nondefensive approach in examining the feasibility of such suggestions.
- To succeed in the modern work arena—with its complex challenges, continuously changing technology, higher employee expectations, and better educated workers—you must move from a management style anchored in obedience—authority to one based on involvement, participation, and commitment.

THE NEW MANAGEMENT CULTURE

Management style can be learned; managers are not born, they are made. Employee participation in management's decision making is an idea whose time has come. Admittedly, the effort to achieve such participation is a time-consuming, difficult, and frustrating endeavor. It means giving up some of your prerogatives. In fact, it means adopting a new management philosophy, involving a shift in power and control, a blurring of the present clear demarcation between managers and subordinates, and efforts to deal with current powerlessness of the average worker. In short, it requires that you begin to treat your subordinates as your allies, not as your enemies.

Frederick Taylor, whose work was the fountainhead of management approaches in the industrial revolution of the early 20th century, held that the work process must be kept independent of the workers' knowledge and depend entirely upon management expertise. By fragmenting formerly unified functions into a myriad of discrete tasks, Taylor's managers gathered unto themselves the knowledge, techniques, and procedures that were once the province of the individual craftsman. This left the workers with little recognition for the work they were doing.

In his *Wealth of Nations*, Adam Smith provides us with a marvelous description of the organization of work in a pin factory—a description that, in some respects, could apply as well to many of the routine chores of the average worker in today's health care institutions:

> One man draws out the wire, another straightens it, a third cuts it, a fourth grinds it at the top for receiving the head; to make the head requires two or three distinct operations; to put it on is a peculiar business, to whiten the pin is another; it is even a trade by itself to put them in the paper; and the important business of making a pin is, in this manner, divided into about eighteen distinct operations . . . all performed by distinct hands.[3]

Smith's description points up the industrial revolution's wholesale transformation of work itself—the division of labor taken to unprecedented extremes.

Workers feel powerless when work is so fragmented. Moreover, the rote performance of routinized tasks makes workers feel alienated. Today, such alienation can be mitigated by bringing workers into the mainstream of planning and decision making. This, however, requires a thorough reorganization of our institutional culture.

Workers want to be involved. You can gain their involvement by sharing your managerial prerogatives, not by hoarding them. This requires constant efforts to reassemble fragmented functions. The result will be the establishment of your own cultural island in the existing organizational structure.

In the coming years, the voices of dissent, the risk takers, who will dare to confront the status quo, will have a major impact on the efficient delivery of health care services. The "protectors of the realm" will be displaced.

Past practices must not be allowed to serve as the rationale for the continuance of such practices. Tomorrow's health care managers must create a new managerial culture—a culture based on innovation!

REFERENCES

1. Rosabeth Moss Kanter, "Forces for Work Improvement in the Public Sector," *QWL Review* (New York State: Committee on Work Environment and Productivity, 1981), 7.

2. Ibid.

3. Adam Smith, *The Wealth of Nations* (New York: Bobbs-Merrill, 1961), 4–5.

Chapter 16

Summing Up: The Call to Excellence

16

We have been told that the human desire for achievement is a critical element in the efficient operation of any institution. We salute managers throughout the health care industry who have an abundance of positive aspirations, yet too often are caught in a vise—oppressed from above and oppressed from below. Why have so many of these managers failed?

We hope this book has sharpened your focus on the elements needed to reverse the trend toward failure and mediocrity. Most of you have been mired in an era in which you have been mesmerized by charting, financial and strategic planning, and cost benefit analysis—to the exclusion of all else. You must now create ways of developing and nurturing the human assets that will tip the scales in favor of excellence. Rather than continue as a captive of scientific management, you must proclaim, ''I'm not going to take this anymore!'' You must, in effect, demand a new *balance of concern*: Let the chartists, the planners, the accountants ''do their thing,'' but insist, from the highest offices of each company and institution, that, finally, ''attention be paid'' to people—to those who breathe life into our charts, plans, projects, and programs. It is time to demystify management.

This book is intended to aid the manager who wants to make things happen but does not know how to, or who has given up because of the institutional environment. It is a book based on hope.

The time has come for managers who kowtow to financial statements, to finally assert themselves and thereby sow the seeds of success. Many of you have felt the frustration of ''thankless days''; you have felt that you were invisible participants in a computerized work arena. Now, you can change that deadening matrix of organizational conformity. You can stop agonizing over the purported loss of the ''work ethic.''

We have sprinkled the previous chapters with a great many tests, exercises, and inventories designed to aid you in your fight against complacency, confrontation,

160

and collapse. Our intent is to change "what's on the shelf" and to shrink the many myths about working people. We have suggested ways to build up an environment of trust. But we have also warned you: surviving is not enough. Thus, we have tried to help you identify the influencers, your potential allies. We have also discussed quick fixes and quick payoffs, while emphasizing that you must be patient. Finally, we have highlighted the essential role that you, as a role model, must play in building up an efficient work force.

Let us review the salient message of the book. Remember the story about the company president who rummaged through his desk for a reward and came up with a banana—the only thing he could immediately put his hands on. If your reaction was, "how bizarre," you missed the point. The president's gesture was in fact a genuine display of recognition and appreciation. Whatever the reward, the very act of rewarding excellent work is likely to result in its repetition. Also, an immediate reward is better than delayed recognition.

When was the last time your boss told you you were doing a good job? When was the last time you did something well, and it was immediately recognized? At such times, you probably experience a sense of elation that lasted not only through the day but for a considerable period of time. Researchers have identified "full appreciation of work done" as number one on the list of employee needs. The reason is obvious: Such appreciation is the missing link in our system. In actuality, we pay too little attention to workers' needs for recognition and appreciation. As the old oriental adage puts it: "If you wish your merit to be known, acknowledge that of other people." Whether you do it with a banana or with some other expression of appreciation, it is essential that you acknowledge your employees' accomplishments *in public*. This satisfies the key need for recognition, for feeling important. It helps employees believe that they are accepted and approved by the institution, and by you.

The key to improving productivity is communicating to employees what is expected of them on the job, day to day, and how well they are doing in meeting those expectations. These are the important points in the critical management process of performance evaluation:[1]

- Work performance is improved appreciably when employees know what results are expected, when they know the methods by which they will be measured, when they know the priorities that have been established.

- Work performance is improved appreciably when employees believe that it is possible to influence the expected results. Too often, cynical employees assume that, no matter what they do, it will not affect the outcome—or the quality of the service.

- The communication of appreciation of the results produced by employees must be clear, specific—and immediate.

The successful health care supervisor is able to communicate reactions to employees who have performed below standard, but is also interested enough to commend those who have performed above standard. In both cases, the supervisor must accept the difficult task of informing people how they are doing.

You, as manager, are responsible for the performance of others, and you must also periodically communicate with them about the results of their performance. You can do this best within an atmosphere or climate of approval, following a four-step procedure:

1. Develop appropriately high performance standards; you do a disservice to both the employee and the institution by setting low standards.
2. Use those standards regularly to measure the employee's performance.
3. Display immediate appreciation for above-par performance.
4. Let below-par performers know that you are aware of their deficiencies and expect their performance to improve.

Whatever their level of employment, workers want to know where they have been, where they are now, and where they are going. Positive reinforcement is essential to show subordinates that they are on the right track. To repeat ourselves: When you reinforce acceptable or exceptional behavior by recognition you will serve to extend such behavior and produce even more acceptable or exceptional behavior.

Health care supervisors must develop new ways of communicating performance results. What is needed is a *plan for progress*, aimed not at perpetuating conformity, nor at institutionalizing criticism, but rather as a basis for providing necessary assistance and improving your employees' performance. It is not the exception, but rather the rule, that employees will agree with their immediate supervisors on the goals of their particular department and also, in the larger picture, on the goals of the institution. In this context, it is the supervisor's responsibility to be an inspiration for improvement. To do this, the supervisor must develop with each worker plans for progress to improve performance and efficiency.

In seeking to change employee attitudes and improve productivity, we tend to rediscover the wheel. Over the years, study after study has directed our attention to the need to *touch* employees. This means getting out from behind our desks, from behind the paperwork, getting our noses out of budget reports, and getting back to where it matters: in face-to-face contact with our employees.

The old monetary reward system, although still satisfying a significant employee need, will not suffice as an incentive to productivity. The values of workers have changed as radically as the workers themselves. We must now pay attention to building up trust.

In today's health care environment, employees still tend to distrust their managers. They tend to be cynical about rewards based upon performance, to feel that, even if they work hard, they will end up "on the short end of the stick."[2] We have to turn around such negative feelings, such lack of trust. However, we cannot do this by analyzing everything again. We cannot do this by concentrating only on policies, organizational structures, job descriptions, or rules and regulations. Though all of these elements are necessary, we, as managers, must concentrate on helping people reach their full potential. We must develop a sense of caring, of appreciation.

In fact, too many workers are alienated on the job. Such alienation is a destructive result of paying too little attention to the supervisor-subordinate relationship, and too much attention to such negative reinforcers as discipline. The alienation results when employees find little or no meaning in their work, no satisfaction from their toils, and no love for the job.

Your employees must know that you care. If they know that you care about them, they will care about you and about their work. The employee-centered supervisor is the one who is less interested in control than in results. Such supervisors attempt to organize and bring together the wealth of human skills available in the work arena.

Who are these employee-centered supervisors? What do they do? Why are they better than others?

- They communicate more. They do not protect information *from* employees; they rather protect employees *with* information.

- They are wonderfully tuned listeners. They are able to respond positively to "silly" questions. They listen to suggestions and complaints with an attitude of fair consideration and willingness to take appropriate actions.

- They are "askers" rather than "tellers." They know that most human beings look for meaning in their work, and find it when their work is appreciated.

Again, to repeat an essential principle: if you treat people as individuals who, like you, need to preserve their integrity and dignity in even the most trying of situations; if you constantly impress them with your concern for their welfare, simply by asking them "why" something has happened; if you let them know when they have done something right, as well as when they have done something wrong; if you let them speak up—then you will not only feel good about yourself, you will also make them feel good about themselves, and about you.

Most of us spend too much time explaining our positions at the expense of understanding where the other person stands. Judicious silence is the hallmark of a good communicator. When you are listening, listen for *feelings*. Pay attention to the *way* the other person says things, as well as to the *what*. Remember, there is no real communication if it is all going one way. Communication is a joint effort. And sound listening habits are contagious; the better listener the supervisor is, the better listening skills that supervisor will inspire.

As a health care supervisor, one of your most difficult responsibilities is to introduce change. The lesson learned from the many studies on productivity is that employees who participate in the shaping of change are more likely to be receptive to that change and, therefore, more productive. If the people who work for you believe that you listen to their suggestions, that you encourage and value their ideas, they are more likely to express their feelings and to make constructive suggestions. The combination of communication, participation, and appreciation marks successful supervision.

Similarly, tasks that are performed through cooperation rather than competition are accomplished more efficiently. In such tasks, the workers exhibit a much higher degree of motivation and morale. In fact, most employees want to be part of a purposeful group. They want to believe that they count. They want to feel that they have a chance to satisfy their needs, to realize their aspirations. The term *feel* is used here intentionally, because perceptions are very important. Indeed, motivation has been described as a function of worker perceptions, of the perceived validity and attainability of various job outcomes.

At the very top of the list of effective supervisory practices is a positive relationship between supervisor and subordinates. To establish such a relationship, supervisors must display a willingness to move from an authority-obedience style of supervision to an involvement-participation-commitment style. The old approaches are not working. The new supervisory style must be aimed primarily at helping people reach their full potential.

It is not enough to say that people are our most important asset. You must display that truth in actions. To enable people to reach their full potential, you must share knowledge, decision making, and credit. You must tell people that you recognize their accomplishments and appreciate their contributions.

If we were asked to list the most important leadership traits—those that would ensure success—the following seven would likely be our choices:

1. a willingness to share power
2. respect for the dignity of others
3. primary concern for the human aspect in management
4. a concern for and attention to the development of subordinates
5. a commitment to rewarding the above average contributor
6. a commitment to tell subordinates when they do not meet standards and to show them how to improve their performance
7. a belief in basic values: human dignity, human fallibility, human needs

When a health care organization is led by managers who view workers, not as instruments of production, but as indispensable resources capable of being motivated and productive under certain working conditions, its key managerial elements—the elements that make up its profile of success—are likely to be:

- an emphasis on organizational informality and fluid, flexible lines of communication and reporting relationships
- a sharing of "managerial prerogatives" with line supervisors and workers on a systematic institutionalized basis
- a managerial ethos that recognizes the importance of the institution's employees
- a system of antiauthoritarian employee relationships and organizational structures that encourage innovation and initiative at the line level

The crisis of work in America is a crisis of management in America. Concern over the purported loss of the "work ethic" cannot obscure the real cause of the crisis: the failure to share responsibility, recognition, and rewards with our employees. The institutions that have escaped the crisis display a sense of caring, managements that listen, and managers who, in their daily dealings with their employees, are concerned with building up trust and commitment. *People-caring* permeates such organizations.

The building up of organizations that take note of the key role played by the individual is the job of the entire management team. In our country's complex hospital management structures, this is not an easy task. Yet it is a task that must be faced. Once we realize that frustration and alienation are the products of inflexible organizational structures in which employees are not allowed to participate in decision making, we can begin to concentrate on the human element and make changes. Bruno Bettelheim has noted that, "if we hope to live not just from moment-to-moment but in true consciousness of our existence, then our greatest need and most difficult achievement is to find meaning in our lives."[3] To find meaning in our lives, we must find meaning in our work. The manager must be the facilitator in that search for meaning.

In our health care institutions, there is a tendency, disturbingly widespread, to believe that the management style we propose—a style that makes the supervisor a collaborative manager rather than a control-centered manager—is too "soft," too concerned with human relations. Several years ago an article in one of the prominent health care magazines defended the authoritarian leader, asserting that benevolent, laid-back administrators were obsolete. In fact, authoritarian leadership has failed, and will continue to fail. Authoritarian leaders may manage to make temporary gains, but in the process they destroy the very heart of the organization.

The managerial heirs of Taylorism, which has heretofore molded administrative structures in both health care and industry, have produced glaring inefficiencies, the list of which is too long to recite here. Yet they continue to proclaim the legitimacy of unshared hegemony over the work process. For them, such hegemony is a sine qua non for managerial success—despite the fact that its exercise makes it almost impossible to motivate the work force. Moreover, these authoritarian leaders display an almost obsessive bias toward measurement and quantitative analysis, comprehensive planning, and policy and procedure manuals. They resist genuine employee-oriented, goal-directed management and continue to act as "quashers of dissent" and blame throwers. But they overlook their own mistakes and failures. The facts are clear: The authoritarian leader breeds alienation; leaders who display a sense of caring have refined their listening antennas and are trust builders who build successful organizations.

A management style that increases self-respect increases efficiency. Thus, a major concern of managers must be to heighten self-respect. In this effort, the collaborative manager should still be forceful; if an employee strays from accepted institutional behavior, the manager must be firm in reacting. Yet, there is no substitute for genuine agreement on the need to do the job the right way. Thus, the challenge for the manager is to find the right handle on employee cooperation.

You must earn cooperative and positive behavior from your employees. You can do this by setting the right example, by displaying a caring attitude, and by being firm, consistent, and fair. You must know your employees personally— their personalities, interests, needs, and concerns. They must believe you care, that you will take the time to deal with them as individuals. Employees still list "help from my supervisor on personal problems" as one of their primary needs.

Thus, respect and care for employee needs must become an essential element in our managerial approach. We must develop a managerial style that has as its basis the following prescription:

> Get to know the people who work for you; get to know them better than you know them now; get them to believe that you care about them as human beings; be the right role model for them.

A productive work force is not created by rules, policies, plans, and budgets. Rather it develops from a set of values that incorporates a respect for people and their contributions to organizational success. If you are a nonthreatening, supportive leader, you will create an attractive work environment and develop a sense of commitment in your subordinates that will have a direct result on the productivity of your department. What follows is a management credo for successful health care supervisors:

1. I shall treat my subordinates as adults. I shall appropriately acknowledge the good works of my subordinates. I shall encourage and recognize excellence.
2. I shall share decision making with my subordinates to the fullest extent possible.
3. I shall listen to dissenters; I shall encourage diversity; I shall change my views when facts are presented which differ from those that I had understood.
4. I shall not pass the buck.
5. I shall, as much as possible, reach out and touch my employees so that they understand that I care.
6. I shall never scapegoat; it is a destructive practice which has negative ramifications.
7. I shall find the fruit of choice in recognizing contributions; some will get a banana, some will get a tangerine, and others a nod of appreciation.

By treating workers fairly, by enunciating and practicing values that recognize the needs, worth, and fears of employees, we do not thereby weaken the productivity and financial validity of the organization. On the contrary, such treatment is certain to enhance productivity and efficiency, because it is based on the simple notion that workers who perform work over which they exercise no control, who produce results that are not recognized, and who feel that they are not part of the organization soon exhibit the classical manifestations of alienation; high absenteeism, low productivity, sullenness, and hostility. The classic response to this that such alienated workers lack discipline and respect for authority or that they are lazy reflects a narrow focus on effects rather than an attempt to understand causes and, therefore, to consider alternate management styles. This traditional response continues to intimidate many of our health care managers and to exact a high price for "over-specialization" and "bottom line management."

To the extent that today's health care managers develop and refine the art of communicating, to that extent they will be effective managers. To the extent they understand *why* employees are more cynical and distrustful than ever before, to that extent they will be the developers of more productive work teams. In fact, health care managers are dealing today with a complex new breed of employees who are far more assertive and knowledgeable about their rights. Managers cannot deal with such employees simply by ordering them to do things. They must rather treat such employees as equals.

Thus, the art of supervision is being reshaped. Old myths are being discarded. Today, the key element in leadership is a genuine interest in people. Those leaders who express a sincere interest in the people who work for them, balancing it with an interest in the work itself, are the most effective.

If you are to do your job properly, gain the respect and admiration of your subordinates, and obtain recognition and rewards from your own superiors, you must see beyond the day-to-day details of your job and develop an understanding of the motivations of your subordinates. You must learn how to speak their language. You must master the techniques of introducing change in the face of resistance. You must replace preplanned subjective evaluation with a greater dependence on facts and a keen appreciation of your subordinate's views and needs. You must build trust and thereby win the participation of all your workers.

The active commitment of employees springs from such a relationship of trust. Managers who listen to their employees and respect and reward their contributions will be rewarded by their employees' commitment. Such managers will use positive reinforcement, delegate responsibility, and communicate regularly with their employees. They will not be concerned only with their own job security and needs; they will realize that, when the worker speaks, "attention must be paid."

Today's health care managers are exposed to conflicting pressures—pressures from above to perpetuate conformity, pressures from below to permit individuality. In the preceding chapters, we have offered you a combination of ideas, propositions, values, and principles that we hope will prompt you to break the grip of these pressures, to liberate yourself, to assert:

> I'M AN IMPORTANT MEMBER OF THE TEAM. I HAVE MUCH TO CONTRIBUTE. I SHOULD BE HEARD. I WILL COOPERATE BUT I WILL NOT SACRIFICE MY INTEGRITY, NOR MY BEING.

REFERENCES

1. Theodore W. Kessler, "Management by Objectives," in *Handbook of Health Care Human Resources Management,* ed. Norman Metzger (Rockville, Md.: Aspen Systems Corporation, 1981), 184–186.

2. David Yankelovich, Address to the National Conference on Human Resources, Dallas, Texas, October 25, 1978.

3. Bruno Bettelheim, *On the Uses of Enchantment: The Meaning and Importance of Fairy Tales* (New York: Knopf Publishing, 1976), 127.

Supervisors' Checklist: It's Time To Take Inventory

CHECKLIST A: FOR DEPARTMENT HEAD LEVEL

This soul-searching exercise is directed toward key management personnel in health care facilities who are responsible for entire departments and, therefore, have other levels of supervision reporting to them. It is a review of some of the material covered earlier. It is a good idea to ask yourself these questions periodically throughout the year.

1. Do you as a department head set the pace and attitudes for your people?
2. Do your people share the job of developing goals?
3. Do you share with your people the goals of the institution?
4. Do you give your people a sense of direction, something to strive for and achieve?
5. Does each member of your department understand the relationship and importance of his or her individual job to the department's operations and to the institution's operations?
6. Do the people in your department understand their responsibilities?
7. Do you endorse the management theory that if subordinates are to plan their course intelligently and work efficiently they need to know the where, what, and why of their jobs: where they are going, what they are doing, and why they are doing it?
8. Do your subordinates have a feeling of being "in" on things?

The authors wish to acknowledge the work of Dr. Leslie M. Slote, industrial psychologist, Hartsdale, N.Y., who developed many of the suggestions for supervisory practices at the various levels.

Source: Reprinted from *The Health Care Supervisor's Handbook,* 2nd edition, by Norman Metzger, pp. 165–169, Aspen Systems Corporation, © 1982.

9. Do you share information or do you keep secrets?
10. Are the supervisors who report to you familiar with top management's thinking, latest institution-wide developments, and the relative importance of various departmental activities to the institution's short- and long-range plans?
11. Do you recognize and accept that it is your responsibility and a priority obligation to keep everyone in your department informed of institutional policy, day-to-day decisions, and most important, reasons for change that affects them as individuals and as work groups?
12. Do your supervisors understand and accept the institution's goals and know how to motivate their subordinates to achieve those goals?
13. Do you notify your people ahead of time of impending changes?
14. Do your requests to your subordinates include the reasons for the requests?
15. Do you have an accurate feedback mechanism?
16. Do you know how your people react to your decisions?
17. Do you know how your people perceive you and the administration?
18. Are you able to cope with rapidly changing situations?
19. Are you able to replan, reorganize, and take emergency action when indicated?
20. Do you have confidence in the people who work for you?
21. Do you indicate such confidence by delegating responsibility with appropriate authority?
22. Are your actions consistent?
23. Are your actions predictable?
24. Do you recognize effort and good work?
25. Do you recognize poor effort and attempt to correct it promptly?
26. Are you convinced that it is just as easy to be positive as to be negative?
27. Do you realize that praise and encouragement often are more productive than criticism?
28. Do your employees feel free to bring problems to you?
29. Have you established a receptive atmosphere for hearing and acting on employee complaints and suggestions?
30. Are you developing understudies from your immediate management level?
31. Is there someone in the department who can replace you if you leave?
32. Do you have a carefully considered supervisory selection and training program for obtaining and developing the type of supervision you want?
33. Do you hold a good person down in one position because he or she is so indispensable there?
34. Do you take a chance on your people by letting them learn through mistakes, by showing a calm reaction and constructive approach to occasional failure, by encouraging them to stick their necks out without fear of the ax, and by instilling self-confidence?

35. Do you use every opportunity to build up in subordinates a sense of the importance of their work?
36. Are you giving real responsibility to your immediate supervisors and then holding them accountable?
37. Do you interfere with jobs of subordinates or do you allow them to exercise discretion and judgment in making decisions?
38. Are you doing things to discourage your subordinates?
39. Are you interested in and aware of the sources of discontentment or discouragement or frustration affecting your supervisors?
40. Do you encourage and listen to the ideas and reactions of your subordinates?
41. Do you give your subordinates credit for their contributions?
42. Do you explain to them why their ideas or suggestions are not acceptable?
43. Do you remember to praise in public but criticize in private?
44. Do you criticize constructively?
45. Are you aware that a feeling of belonging builds self-confidence and makes people want to work harder than ever?
46. Do you show your people a future?
47. Are you aware of the fact that maximum self-development always takes place when a person feels, understands, accepts, and exercises the full weight of responsibility for his or her job?

CHECKLIST B: FOR INTERMEDIATE-LEVEL SUPERVISORS

You are in a position where you report to a department head and have first-line supervisors reporting to you. Refer to this checklist throughout the year to gauge your effectiveness.

1. Do you have a thorough understanding of institutional goals, your part in meeting budgets, and do you have full confidence in their attainment?
2. Do you offer suggestions or constructive criticism to your supervisor (the department head) and ask for additional information when necessary?
3. Do you build team spirit and group pride by getting everyone into the act of setting goals and pulling together?
4. Do you deal with emergencies as they come up, or do you have scheduled times for meetings with your department head and with your first-line supervisors?
5. Do you encourage each of your supervisors to come up with suggestions on ways to improve things?
6. When you do not accept your supervisors' suggestions, do you explain why?

7. Have you set up an atmosphere that enables your subordinates to approach you with job or personal problems?
8. Do people believe that you listen empathetically and really care about their problems?
9. Do you keep your supervisors informed on how they are doing?
10. Do you give credit where credit is due and offer constructive criticism when necessary?
11. Do your supervisors appear to be too busy with work problems to be concerned about their employees' personal difficulties?
12. Does your example encourage your supervisors to build individual worker confidence and praise good performance?
13. Do your supervisors know that you expect them to communicate to their people how jobs are evaluated and what the job rates and progressions are?
14. Do your supervisors keep their people informed of promotional opportunities?
15. Do your supervisors train their people for better jobs?

CHECKLIST C: FOR IMMEDIATE/FIRST-LINE SUPERVISORS

As a first-line supervisor you should review the following checklist on a regular basis.

1. Do you know that good communication means being available to answer employee questions?
2. Do you accept employees' need to know what is expected of them, how well they are doing their jobs, and how they will be rewarded for good work?
3. Have you permitted your employees freedom and latitude in performing their work, or are you constantly supervising employees?
4. Are you personally interested in the well-being of the people who work for you?
5. Do you recommend good workers for promotions, merit increases, and other forms of recognition?
6. Do you consult with your employees and permit them to share in the decision-making process?
7. Do you realize that pent-up emotions are dangerous and, therefore, do you provide an accessible sounding board for employee complaints and grievances?
8. Do you ever say or do anything that detracts from the sense of personal dignity that each of your people has?

9. When a job is well done do you praise the worker, and when a job is done poorly do you criticize constructively?
10. Do you realize that people want to feel important?
11. Do you realize that people want recognition?
12. Do you realize that people want credit and attention?
13. Do you realize that people have their own self-interest at heart?
14. Do you realize that people want to be better off tomorrow than today?
15. Do you realize that people want prompt action on their questions?
16. Do you realize that people would rather talk than listen?
17. Do you realize that people would rather give advice than take advice?
18. Do you realize that people generally resent too-close supervision?
19. Do you realize that people resent change?
20. Do you realize that people are naturally curious?
21. Do you ask questions instead of giving orders?
22. Do you make suggestions instead of giving orders?
23. Do you keep in mind the employees' self-interest?
24. Do you make your employees feel that their work is useful?
25. Do you make your employees feel that they are trusted members of the work group?
26. Do you represent your employees' interests to the next level of supervision?
27. Do you represent the management to your employees?
28. Are you too busy with work problems to be concerned with employees' personal difficulties?
29. Do you look for and find opportunities to praise and reward a good performance, or are you afraid of being accused of sentimentality and coddling?
30. Are you consistent or do you play favorites?
31. Are you predictable or do your employees feel they never know what your next move will be?
32. Do you try to rotate your people and build up skills for individual flexibility within the group?
33. Do you spend enough time training your people?
34. Do you understand the problem with legislating change rather than selling change?
35. Do your employees perceive you as a "people-centered" supervisor?
36. Do your employees trust you?

Motivation Feedback Questionnaire

Part I

Questions

Directions: The following statements have seven possible responses.

Strongly Agree	Agree	Slightly Agree	Don't Know	Slightly Disagree	Disagree	Strongly Disagree
+3	+2	+1	0	−1	−2	−3

Please score each statement by circling the number that corresponds to your response. For example, if you "strongly agree," circle the number +3.

1. Special salary increases should be given to employees who do their jobs well.   +3 +2 +1   0 −1 −2 −3
2. Better job descriptions would be helpful so that employees know exactly what is expected of them.   +3 +2 +1   0 −1 −2 −3
3. Employees need to be reminded that their jobs are dependent upon the group's ability to meet its objective.   +3 +2 +1   0 −1 −2 −3
4. Supervisors should give a great deal of attention to the physical working conditions of their employees.   +3 +2 +1   0 −1 −2 −3

Source: Reprinted from *Effective Communication in Health Care* by Harry E. Munn, Jr., and Norman Metzger, pp. 215–217, Aspen Systems Corporation, © 1981.

5. Supervisors ought to work hard to develop a friendly working atmosphere among their employees.   +3 +2 +1   0 −1 −2 −3

6. Individual recognition for above-standard performance means a lot to employees.   +3 +2 +1   0 −1 −2 −3

7. Indifferent supervision can often bruise feelings.   +3 +2 +1   0 −1 −2 −3

8. Employees want to feel that their real skills and capacities are put to use on their jobs.   +3 +2 +1   0 −1 −2 −3

9. The group's retirement benefits and medical insurance programs are important factors in keeping employees on their jobs.   +3 +2 +1   0 −1 −2 −3

10. Almost every job can be made more stimulating and challenging.   +3 +2 +1   0 −1 −2 −3

11. Many employees want to give their best in everything they do.   +3 +2 +1   0 −1 −2 −3

12. Management could show more interest in the employees by sponsoring social events after hours.   +3 +2 +1   0 −1 −2 −3

13. Pride in one's work is actually an important reward.   +3 +2 +1   0 −1 −2 −3

14. Employees want to think of themselves as the "best" at their jobs.   +3 +2 +1   0 −1 −2 −3

15. The quality of the relationship in the informal work group is quite important.   +3 +2 +1   0 −1 −2 −3

16. Individual merit raises would improve the performance of employees.   +3 +2 +1   0 −1 −2 −3

17. Visibility with upper management is important to employees.   +3 +2 +1   0 −1 −2 −3

18. Employees generally like to schedule their own work and make job-related decisions with a minimum of supervision.   +3 +2 +1   0 −1 −2 −3

19. Job security is important to employees.   +3 +2 +1   0 −1 −2 −3

20. Having good equipment to work with is important to employees.   +3 +2 +1   0 −1 −2 −3

Motivation Feedback Questionnaire
Part II
Scoring

1. Enter the numbers you circled in Part I in the blanks below after the appropriate statement number.

Statement No.	Score	Statement No.	Score
10	___	2	___
11	___	3	___
13	___	9	___
18	___	19	___
SELF-ACTUALIZATION ___Total		SAFETY ___Total	

Statement No.	Score	Statement No.	Score
6	___	1	___
8	___	4	___
14	___	16	___
17	___	20	___
ESTEEM ___Total		BASIC___Total	

Statement No.	Score
5	___
7	___
12	___
15	___
BELONGINGNESS ___Total	

2. Record your scores in the chart by putting an "X" in each row under the number of your total score for that area of need-motivation. After you have completed this chart, you can see the relative strength of your response to each area of "need-motivation." There is of course no "right" answer. What motivates you might not motivate someone else. In general, however, most motivational theorists believe that most employees are motivated by managers who stress the belongingness and esteem needs of their employees.

Motivation Feedback Questionnaire
Part II
(continued)

DEGREE OF EMPHASIS	−12	−10	−8	−6	−4	−2	0	+2	+4	+6	+8	+10	+12
Self-Actualization													
Esteem													
Belongingness													
Safety													
Basic													

LOW USE   HIGH USE

Semantic-Differential Test

SEE YOURSELF
AS YOUR EMPLOYEES SEE YOU

It takes courage to give and take this test.
But the results may help your company to
function more harmoniously.

Ever wonder what your executives really think of you and whether your relations with them are all that they should be? I've devised a simple method for finding out both these things.

I've employed it in businesses, hospitals, and government. I've used it at the highest levels of management and at the lowest. And everywhere I've used it, it's been enthusiastically received. In fact, whenever I've suggested discontinuing its use, I've usually stirred up a storm of protest.

The method involves the use of a so-called semantic-differential test. Don't let the fancy name throw you. The test is both easy to give and to score. Here's how it works.

On one side of a single sheet of paper, I've listed 20 sets of adjectives or phrases. Each set contains two adjectives or phrases of exactly opposite meaning. Thus: competent and incompetent, cold and warm, leader and follower, sincere and insincere, closed-minded and open-minded, solves problems and ignores problems, restricts others and permits initiative.

Source: Reprinted with permission of Leslie M. Slote, Management Consultant, Hartsdale, New York. Previously published in *Business Management,* May 1966.

Between each of these polar adjectives or phrases are seven blank spaces. These give each person who takes the test seven choices. Thus, to take one example, he can rate himself (or others) very competent, quite competent or slightly competent. Or he can rate himself (or others) slightly incompetent, quite incompetent, or very incompetent. Or he can indicate that he has no opinion and check a blank space in the middle of the page.

HOW THE TEST WORKS

I give this test to people in groups. Usually, the group numbers from 10 to 20 people and consists of, say, a top-level executive and the people right under him, or a department head and the people right under him, or a group of people entirely on the same level.

I give each person a form to rate himself and separate forms to rate everyone else in the room.

I then ask one member of the group to fill in the form as he sees himself. Simultaneously, I ask all other members of the group to fill in their forms as they see him.

Once everyone is through, I shuffle the forms filled out by the group and hand them to the person being rated. He can see, at a few glances, how the group's opinion of him differs from his own. If he wishes, he can even chart his reaction and the composite reaction of the group.

There are tremendous advantages to this test. But before I get into them, let me tell you of some of the disadvantages and of how group estimates of an individual commonly coincide with or diverge from the individual's estimate of himself.

Obviously, there is some similarity between a group's estimate of a man and his own estimate of himself. We wouldn't be rational if this weren't the case.

Thus, I've found that the group and the individual are inclined to agree rather well on how competent the individual is. They're also inclined to agree on how high or low his morale is and whether he's warm or cold or friendly or unfriendly.

In the case of some of the other adjectives and phrases, however, there's apt to be disagreement. Thus, I've found that people tend to see themselves as being more approachable than others see them. They also think they're better listeners than others think they are. And they tend to think of themselves as having greater leadership qualities than others do. Perhaps worst of all, they tend to believe they're more sincere than they are commonly regarded.

SOME GET MAD

All of which brings me to the one big disadvantage of the semantic-differential test. When confronted with others' opinions of them, some people blow up. One administrator I know took this test and rated herself as quite a good leader. But the people under her rated her as somewhat of a follower and fence straddler. That made her boiling mad, and she actually got into a fight about it with the people who had rated her.

Or take the supervisor who thought of himself as very sincere. His fellow workers rated him as being somewhat insincere. At the time, he and the people who had rated him were being trained as supervisors, and he was so mad that he refused to go back to the training sessions. "The hell with those people," he said.

The group responded by saying, "This is how we honestly feel about him, and we'll be glad to talk it over with him if he wants to come back." So far, he hasn't. He doesn't want to face the group—or himself.

The test has at least two other disadvantages. The first is that the test is limited. No group of adjectives, whether they number 20 or 120, can do full justice to an individual. At best, they can highlight a few aspects of his personality that seem significant in his relations with others.

The second is that the test is a little less effective at high levels of management than at low ones. Even though everyone hands in his filled-in form anonymously, people at the top levels of management seem to have more concerns and inhibitions than people lower down. This is not to say that they don't take to the test. They most certainly do—but just a little less enthusiastically than, say, a typical middle manager.

So much for the test's limitations. What are its advantages?

First and foremost, it helps a person to improve his ability to communicate. We all have fond images of how we think we get across to other people. We also have idealized images of how we'd like to get across to them. Both these images are self-deceptions if they don't correspond with how we actually do get across. So, if an executive finds that most of the people he works with consider him somewhat gutless and insincere, he can ponder his behavior.

Second, the test can help an individual improve his general relations with a group. Many people who take the test want to discuss the results with other members of their group, and I do everything I can to encourage this. It helps clear the air—as well as improve behavior—if a person finds out why he impresses others in a certain way.

To this end, I often ask a group to circle just one or two of the adjectives they've checked—one or two that they think the individual involved ought to pay special attention to. The adjectives may be either favorable or unfavorable. If the latter, this special emphasis not only helps mitigate the individual's concern about what may be sweepingly unfavorable group judgments, but also helps him focus his efforts at self-improvement. It tells him what he should be most concerned about.

It's also useful for an individual to talk over the results of his test if various persons have rated him quite differently. Widely diverse ratings don't show up too often. Usually, a group's judgment is quite consistent. But disagreement within a group does occur occasionally. And it gives a man food for thought if he finds out that one or two persons consider him, say, quite insincere, while others view him differently. He usually wants to find out why he is impressing one or two so differently.

One other benefit of group discussions: Most people view other people as being more satisfied than they actually are. But frustrated individuals—and most people seem to be frustrated, to one degree or another—don't sound off about it. They keep it within themselves. As a result, their frustration drains their energy and undermines their on-the-job effectiveness.

But when this frustration is brought out in a group, the problems that are causing it can sometimes be solved. Or the individual can be made to look at them in a different light.

Third, the test sometimes helps bolster people's confidence. This isn't always the case. As I've already indicated, most people tend to rate themselves more highly than their peers do, especially in the areas of approachability, leadership, and sincerity. But, occasionally, a man doesn't have as good an image of himself as he should have, and the test does wonders for his morale.

A HAPPIER MAN

Take a foreman in an industrial plant in the Northeast. He rated himself significantly less competent, less bright, less approachable, less of a leader, and less constructive than his peers rated him. The differences were so sharp that I asked him if we could discuss them with the group, and he readily agreed. The other people told him to his face that they thought he had a lot on the ball—more than he gave himself credit for. And when he took his own form and the group's composite form home to his wife, she told him the same thing. Result: a happier man.

There's a fourth advantage to the semantic-differential test. It can be used not only to test individuals but also to test organizations or any particular units in an organization. Among other sets of adjectives that can be employed in this connection are the following: secure/insecure, trustful/mistrustful, feelings ignored/ feelings shared, and decisions from above/shared decisions.

Obviously, use of the test in this way can be particularly useful in firms that experience a high rate of employee turnover. Just by pinpointing conditions that cause employee chagrin, a company can take a big step toward improving its working atmosphere.

NINE POINTERS

Now, if you want to use the test in your firm, either on individuals or on the climate in the company, here are some tips I've derived from occasionally hard-won experience.

1. Always have people fill out the forms in a group rather than at their desks. A person who fills out the form in a group has less fear than a person who fills it out alone—and is more apt to give honest answers. (It goes almost without saying that you should assure your employees that the test will not be used against them in any way.)

2. Always make sure your group is of reasonably good size. A good size is 10 to 15. And only rarely should there be fewer than 8. When there are fewer, fear of discovery increases.

3. Always make sure that everyone fills out the form in the same way. Have them all use pencils, preferably of the same kind. And have them all make the same kind of checkmark. This procedure also helps lessen fear of discovery.

4. If you are the leader of the group, make sure you are rated along with everyone else. In fact, no one should be excluded without good reason. If anyone is excluded, the others will think it's not fair.

5. Try to confine any one testing to a certain level or segment of management. The farther apart groups of people are in a company hierarchy, the less valid their judgments of each other. Thus, one company I dealt with asked all its employees to give their opinion of top management in general. Result: The people closest to top management had a very realistic view. Those much farther down the line had a rather glorified view.

6. Don't consider my list of polar adjectives sacrosanct. I think it's a good list because I've compiled it after learning what employees at many different organizations considered the most pertinent terms for describing people. But other adjectives can certainly be substituted or added. Some possibilities: considerate/ inconsiderate, cautious/impulsive, dominant/submissive and stable/unstable.

7. If you do dream up other sets of adjectives, try them out on a few key people in advance. You should all agree on the meaning of the words or you will throw your results off. Prior agreement on the meaning and pertinence of adjectives is especially important if you want to test an organization's climate.

8. Don't spend too much time on the test. If you have 15 people and 15 sets of adjectives, you can give the test to all 15 in 35 or 40 minutes. And it's to your advantage to do so. The faster people check off their opinions, the more valid the results. Remember, this test does not necessarily reveal the absolute truth about a person. It reveals the relative truth about him—namely, the impressions he makes on others.

9. Hold follow-up meetings. Once people have the results of the test, encourage them to chart their opinions of themselves against the group's composite opinion. Then, hold one or more follow-up meetings so individuals can discuss discrepancies of particular interest or concern to them. Remember, this test is not to be given just for the fun of it. It's to be given with the aim of improving relations between individuals and a group—particularly the ability of any one individual to communicate with the group. And to achieve this aim, you should discuss the results.

Nonetheless, the test is fun—for most people. A few, to be sure, get irritated, even angry. But most come back for more, even when it hurts a bit.

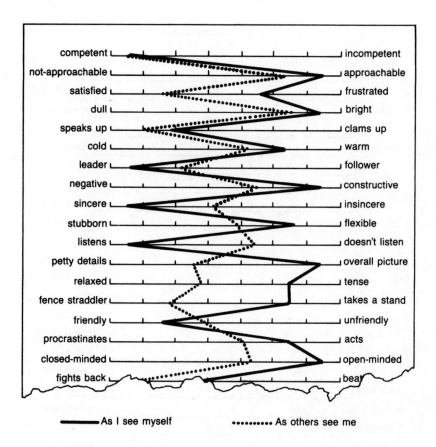

competent — incompetent
not-approachable — approachable
satisfied — frustrated
dull — bright
speaks up — clams up
cold — warm
leader — follower
negative — constructive
sincere — insincere
stubborn — flexible
listens — doesn't listen
petty details — overall picture
relaxed — tense
fence straddler — takes a stand
friendly — unfriendly
procrastinates — acts
closed-minded — open-minded
fights back — beat

⎯⎯⎯ As I see myself   •••••••• As others see me

How to score the test. You can score the ratings other people give you—and chart these ratings, too. Here's how: (1) Take a blank form and fill in the number of check marks other people made in each of the seven blank spaces. Do this for each set of adjectives. (2) Number the spaces one through seven, moving from left to right. (3) Multiply the number of checks in each space by the number of the space. Thus, if there are two check marks in the first space, the total is two (one times two). If there are four in the second, the total is eight (two times four). And so forth. Then, total these figures. (4) Divide the resulting figure by the number of people who rated you. Thus, if the total figure for competent/incompetent comes to 23 and you were rated by nine people, your weighted average for this category would be 2.6. This would indicate that other people are roughly divided between thinking you are quite competent and slightly competent. (5) Jot down your weighted average for each category at the far right of the tally sheet. (6) Plot these weighted averages on graph paper or on a blank form, and connect the points you plot. Remember that the slopes of the lines have no meaning—only their end points. (7) Finally, plot the ratings you gave yourself. Result: a chart that quickly shows major discrepancies between your opinions of yourself and the opinions that other executives or your employees hold about you.

Semantic-Differential Test

	VERY	QUITE	SLIGHT		SLIGHT	QUITE	VERY	
competent:	:	:	:	:	:	:	:incompetent
not approachable:	:	:	:	:	:	:	:approachable
satisfied:	:	:	:	:	:	:	:frustrated
dull:	:	:	:	:	:	:	:bright
speaks up:	:	:	:	:	:	:	:clams up
cold:	:	:	:	:	:	:	:warm
leader:	:	:	:	:	:	:	:follower
negative:	:	:	:	:	:	:	:constructive
sincere:	:	:	:	:	:	:	:insincere
stubborn:	:	:	:	:	:	:	:flexible
listens:	:	:	:	:	:	:	:doesn't listen
petty details:	:	:	:	:	:	:	:over-all picture
relaxed:	:	:	:	:	:	:	:tense
fence straddler:	:	:	:	:	:	:	:takes a stand
friendly:	:	:	:	:	:	:	:unfriendly
procrastinates:	:	:	:	:	:	:	:acts
closed-minded:	:	:	:	:	:	:	:open-minded
fights back:	:	:	:	:	:	:	:beaten down
gets to point:	:	:	:	:	:	:	:roundabout
receptive:	:	:	:	:	:	:	:closed
emotional:	:	:	:	:	:	:	:objective
helps others:	:	:	:	:	:	:	:ignores others
unfair:	:	:	:	:	:	:	:permits initiative
solves problems:	:	:	:	:	:	:	:ignores problems
restricts others:	:	:	:	:	:	:	:permits initiative
sees both sides:	:	:	:	:	:	:	:sees one side
clear:	:	:	:	:	:	:	:vague
guts:	:	:	:	:	:	:	:gutless

How to take the test: Whether you are rating yourself or others, you can give one of seven different ratings for any one category. A glance at the test reveals six of the seven. The seventh is "No opinion," indicated by marking the middle column.

List of Quotations

p. ix   "A generation of . . ."
           Source: Seymour Melman, *Dynamic Factors in Industrial Productivity* (London: Blackwell, 1956), 97.

p. ix   "Survival in an . . ."
           Source: Samuel B. Bacharach and Edward J. Lawler, *Power and Politics in Organizations* (San Francisco: Jossey-Bass, 1981), 1.

p. 1   "In Hegel's view . . ."
           Source: Anatole Broyard, "On Authority," *New York Times*, Sunday, 2 January 1983), Book Review section.

p. 17   "Competition for the . . ."
           Source: Earl Shorris, *The Oppressed Middle: Politics of Middle Management* (Garden City, N.Y.: Anchor Press/Doubleday, 1981), 229.

p. 20   "We can establish . . ."
           Source: Ernst Becker, *The Denial of Death* (New York: The Free Press/Macmillan, 1973), 144.

p. 22   "I have steadily . . ."
           Source: Charles Darwin

p. 22   "It does not . . ."
           Source: José Ortega y Gasset, *The Revolt of the Masses* (New York: Norton Publishing, 1957), 156–157.

p. 23　"If we hope . . ."
Source: Bruno Bettelheim, On the Uses of Enchantment (New York: Random House, 1977), 48.

p. 24　"Self-reliant, trusting, and . . ."
Source: Robert N. McMurry, "Clear Communications for Chief Executives," Harvard Business Review, March/April 1965: 131.

p. 27　"Our general observation . . ."
Source: Thomas J. Peters and Robert H. Waterman, Jr., In Search of Excellence (New York: Harper & Row, 1983), 70.

p. 28　"Late one evening . . ."
Source: Thomas J. Peters and Robert H. Waterman, Jr., In Search of Excellence (New York, Harper & Row, 1983), 70–71.

p. 31　"If you wish . . ."
Source: Old oriental adage

p. 33　"What one person . . ."
Source: N. McGeehee and P.W. Thayer, Training in Business and Industry (New York: John Wiley & Sons, 1960), 140.

p. 37　"There is sometimes . . ."
Source: Robert M. Fulmer, The New Management, 3rd ed. (New York: Macmillan, 1983), 242.

p. 45　"In effect, the . . ."
Source: Michael Maccoby, The Leader (New York: Ballantine Books, 1981), 49.

p. 53　"Andrew Carnegie once . . ."
Source: James J. Cribbin, Effective Managerial Leadership (New York: AMACOM, Division of American Management Associations, 1983), 191.

p. 61　"If managers are . . ."
Source: James J. Hayes, Memos for Management Leadership (New York: AMACOM, Division of American Management Associations, 1983), 105.

p. 73   "You punish the . . ."
          Source: Protagoras

p. 81   "In essence, what . . ."
          Source: Richard S. Ruch and Ronald Goodman, *Image at the Top*
          (New York: Free Press/Macmillan, 1983), 61.

p. 83   "Ordinary people are . . ."
          Source: John Naisbitt, "A New Era of Opportunity," *Success*, April
          1985, 38.

p. 84   "Industrial democracy. This . . ."
          Source: James L. Hayes, *Memos for Management* (New York:
          AMACOM, Division of American Management Associa-
          tions, 1983), 14.

p. 86   "If a worker . . ."
          Source: William Foote White, et al., *Worker Participation and
          Ownership* (Ithaca, NY: ILR Press, Cornell University,
          1983), 120.

p. 87   "Japanese senior management . . ."
          Source: James S. Balloun, director of McKinsey & Co., *New York
          Times*, 12 July 1981, op ed page.

p. 89   "Trust your employees . . ."
          Source: Robert E. Cole, *Work Mobility and Participation: Com-
          parative Study of American and Japanese Industry*
          (University of California Press, 1979), p. 76

p. 91   "Have positive outlook . . ."
          Source: J. Hall, *New York Times*, 18 September 1981, op ed page.

p. 92   "Help thy brother's . . ."
          Source: Hindu proverb

p. 93   "Change is inevitable . . ."
          Source: Benjamin Disraeli

p. 103   "The successful change . . ."
          Source: Gordon L. Lippitt, Petter Langseth, and Jack Mossop, *Imple-
          menting Organizational Change* (San Francisco: Jossey-
          Bass, 1985), 166–167.

p. 117   "Dost thou love . . ."
           Source: Benjamin Franklin

p. 131   "The man who . . ."
           Source: Raymond F. Valentine, *Performance Objectives for Manag-
           ers* (New York: American Management Associations, 1966),
           208.

p. 139   "A manager who . . ."
           Source: Earl Shorris, *The Oppressed Middle: Politics of Middle Man-
           agement* (Garden City, N.Y.: Anchor Press/Doubleday,
           1981), 373.

p. 140   "The inability of . . ."
           Source: Gail Sheehy, *Pathfinders* (New York: William Morrow &
           Co., 1981), 266–267.

p.143–144 "The Calf Path . . ."
           Source: Sam Walter Foss

p. 151   "The ways in . . ."
           Source: Harley Shaiken, *Work Transformed: Automation & Labor in
           the Computer Age* (New York: Holt, Rinehart & Winston,
           1984), xii.

p. 151   "Participation is not . . ."
           Source: Simmons and Mares, *Working Together* (New York: Alfred
           A. Knopf, 1983), 3.

p. 179   "See yourself as . . ."
           Source: Leslie Slote, "See Yourself As Your Employees See You,"
           Business Management, May 1966, Council section.

Index

About the Authors

Lawrence C. Bassett is a founder, principal, and President of Professional Services of Applied Leadership Technologies, Inc. His experience as a Certified Management Consultant includes work with industry, retailing, health care, and government organizations. Before becoming a consultant in 1966, he held a number of important staff and line positions. He is experienced in the full range of employee/labor relations, organizational development, and personnel administration.

In recent years, Mr. Bassett has developed several novel and effective approaches to management training. In addition, he has researched and designed approaches that offer practical answers to a number of important problems inherent in today's management environment, including those involved in measuring and increasing employee productivity and improving interpersonal relationships between and among employees and between company personnel and the public.

Mr. Bassett is a frequent speaker and writer. He is on the graduate school faculties of New York University and Fairleigh Dickinson University and has been a guest lecturer at the Columbia University School of Public Health and Administrative Medicine. He is also a member of the National Panel of the American Arbitration Association.

In his involvement with professional societies, Mr. Bassett has served as both vice-president and member of the board of directors of the Society of Professional Management Consultants. He holds BA and MBA degrees from New York University.

Norman Metzger occupies an endowed chair, the Edmond A. Guggenheim Professorship, in the Department of Health Care Management at the Mount Sinai School of Medicine and is vice-president for labor relations at the Mount Sinai Medical Center in New York City. He is also an adjunct professor in both the Management Graduate Program in Health Care Administration at the Bernard M.

Baruch College of the City University of New York and the Graduate Program in Health Services Administration at the New School for Social Research.

Mr. Metzger has written close to 100 articles on the subjects of motivation, labor relations, evaluation of employee performance, recruitment, orientation, job evaluation, communication, discipline, and, most recently, as a result of extensive research, on the issues of changing leadership styles and worker participation. His latest research is in the area of changing worker attitudes and on the new breed of supervisor.

Mr. Metzger is a five-time recipient of the annual award for literature given by the American Society of Hospital Personnel Administration in recognition of his outstanding contribution to hospital personnel administration literature. He is the author, coauthor, or editor of eleven books.